Grammar Based English

For beginners

KB180766

우종현(Jonghyeon Woo)

○ 영문학 박사
○ 백석문화대학교 교수
○ 한국영어어문교육학회 이사

Grammar Based **English**

© 우종현, 2016
1판 1쇄 인쇄_2016년 03월 02일
1판 1쇄 발행_2016년 03월 10일

지은이_우종현
펴낸이_이종엽
펴낸곳_글모아출판
　　　등록_제324-2005-42호

공급처_(주)글로벌콘텐츠출판그룹
　　　대표_홍정표　**이사**_양정섭
　　　편집_노경민 송은주　**디자인**_김미미　**기획·마케팅**_노경민　**경영지원**_안선영
　　　주소_서울특별시 강동구 천중로 196 정일빌딩 401호
　　　전화_02) 488-3280　**팩스**_02) 488-3281
　　　홈페이지_http://www.gcbook.co.kr

값 12,000원
ISBN 978-89-94626-40-6 93740

Grammar Based Based English

For beginners

우종현 지음

글모아출판

　이 책은 초급대학 수준의 학습자들을 위한 기초적인 영어 학습서이기 때문에 영어에 흥미를 갖지 못해 영어책만 보아도 머리가 아프거나, 영어에 대한 두려움을 갖고 있는 학습자들이 편하게 학습할 수 있는 내용으로 엮어졌다.

　제시된 단어들은 일상생활에 자주 사용되는 기초적인 단어로서, 주제별로 학습할 수 있도록 했다.

　각 단원별 제시되고 있는 영어 문법 내용은 영문법에서 제시하고 있는 모든 영역을 다루고 있다. 특히, 가장 기본적이고 핵심적인 문법 내용을 복잡한 문장이나 어려운 단어들을 피하여 설명함으로써, 학습자들이 쉽게 학습할 수 있도록 했다.

contents

Family Relationship

father	mother
son	daughter
grand father	grand mother
brother	sister
aunt	uncle
niece	nephew
cousin	
mother in law	father in law
son in law	daughter in law
brother in law	sister in law

Tell me about your family.

Alice: You look different. Oh, I know. Your dress is very beautiful.

Emma: Thanks. My sister presented it to me for my birthday.

Alice: How old is she?

Emma: She is 23. Look, here is a photo of us together.

Alice: You really look alike! And who's that?

Emma: That's my brother Bill. He is a teacher.

Alice: Is he married?

Emma: Yes, he is. He has two children. I love them very much.

Alice: You look too young to be an aunt!

Emma: So, tell me about your family. Do you have any brothers and sisters?

Alice: Yes, I have two brothers, but no sisters. They are all older than me.

 **Pattern Practice**

Who is she/he?

He/She is my _____.

Do you have any _____ and _____?

I have _____ and _____.

How old he/she is?

My _____ is _____ years old.

아빠 _____   엄마 _____

아들 _____   딸 _____

할아버지 _____   할머니 _____

남자형제 _____   여자형제 _____

고모/이모 _____ (외)삼촌 _____

여자조카 _____   남자조카 _____

사촌 _____

장모/시어머니 _____   장인/시아버지 _____

사위 _____   며느리 _____

매형/매제 _____   처형/처제 _____

_____.

_____.

의미: 다른 나라 언어와 마찬가지로, 영어 문장이 되기 위해서는 일정한 구조적인 규칙을 가지고 있으며, 이 규칙에 따라 문장을 사용할 때 비로써 의미를 확정한다.

1. 문장의 구성요소 및 성분

1) 문장의 구성 요소: 단어, 구, 절

단어: 말의 최소 단위로서 영어에서는 그 특성(품사)에 따라 8가지로 구분

I love peace.

구(Phrase): 두 개 이상의 단어가 한 덩어리가 되어 의미를 갖는 것

My mother takes care of many children.

절(Clause): 두 개 이상의 단어가 한 덩어리가 되어 의미를 가지면서, 주어와 동사(술어)관계가 있는 것

I think the boy is honest.

 * **단어의 특성(품사)**

명사: 사람, 사물 등 유·무형을 지칭

예) book, family, love, water, Seoul

대명사: 명사를 대신해서 받는 것

예) I, you, he, she, they, we, it

동사: 동작이나 상태를 나타내는 것

예) go, come, run, study, see, eat

형용사: 명사의 성질이나 상태를 나타냄

예) beautiful, good, kind, happy, honest

부사: 여러 다른 품사의 상태를 나타내고, 장소, 방법, 시간, 이유 등을 표현

예) very, pretty, easily, fast, happily

접속사: 단어와 단어, 구와 구, 절과 절 등을 연결

예) and, or, but, that, because

전치사: 명사를 목적어로 해서 기본 문장을 확장

예) in, at, on, from, for

감탄사: 놀람이나 감탄을 나타낸다.

예) wow, oh

2) 문장 성분: 문장에서 어떤 쓰임을 하느냐에 따라 주어, 술어(동사), 목적어, 보어 등으로 구분하는데 이를 문장 성분이라 한다.

주어: 문장의 주체로서 '은/는/이/가'로 해석

동사(술어): 문장을 서술해 주는 것으로서 '~다'로 해석

보어: 주어나 목적어를 설명하는 것

목적어: 주어 행위의 대상으로서 '~에게' 또는 '을/를'로 해석

I painted the door green.

(I: 주어, painted: 동사, the door: 목적어, green: 보어)

2. 문장의 기본 구조(문장의 5가지 형태)

　모든 영어 문장은 5가지 구조를 가지고 있는데, 이것을 문장의 5형식이라고 하며 1형식문장, 2형식문장, 3형식문장, 4형식문장, 5형식문장이라고 각각 말해진다.

1) 1형식: 주어 + 동사(Subject + Verb)

The sun rises in the east every morning.

Birds sing in the forest.

Tom is not here.

My father works at the school.

2) 2형식: 주어 + 동사 + 보어(S + V + Complement)

I will be nineteen next summer.

I am very happy.

He became a doctor.

The report proved false.

She looks happy.

She appears sensible.

* 대표적인 2형식 동사

be, become, go, grow, get, look, appear, seem, remain

3) 3형식: 주어 + 동사 + 목적어(S + V + Object)

I like a love story.

I met him at the campus.

They helped the old man.

I finished the project.

4) 4형식: 주어 + 동사 + 간접목적어 + 직접목적어
(S + V + O + Indirect Object + Direct Object)

I gave her the book.

→ I gave the book to her. (3형식)

He sent the patient flowers.

→ He sent flowers to the patient. (3형식)

Linda teaches us English.

→ Linda teaches English to us. (3형식)

* 4형식을 3형식으로 고칠 때 to를 사용하지 않는 동사

buy, build, make, get, order, cook, receive: for + I.O.

I'll make some coffee for you.

ask, require, beg, demand, inquire: of + I.O.

He asked a question of me.

play, impose, bestow, confer: on + I.O.

He played a trick on me.

They imposed a tax of 100 dollars on me.

5) 5형식: 주어 + 동사 + 목적어 + 보어(S + V + O + C)

We elected him president.

I found this book easy.

I painted the desk blue.

They believed the boy honest.

3. 동사의 종류

동사를 분류하는 데는 다양한 방법이 있는데, 문장을 만들 때는 동사(술어)가 그 다음에 오는 문장 성분을 선택하게 된다. 따라서 문장을 만들 때에는 동사의 선택이 중요하며, 동사의 선택에 따라 문장이 구분되어 만들어 진다.

자동사: 목적어를 선택하지 않는 동사

The earth <u>moves</u> round the sun. (1형식)

She <u>became</u> a famous singer. (2형식)

타동사: 목적어를 선택하는 동사

I don't <u>know</u> the doctor. (3형식)

The boy <u>sent</u> the girl a present. (4형식)

We <u>called</u> him a fool. (5형식)

Exercise

A. 밑줄 친 단어의 품사를 구분하세요.

1. I forgot to book a <u>ticket</u> for the movie.

2. I am going to meet him <u>at</u> the coffee shop.

3. Mary <u>and</u> Tom look very happy.

4. He showed her an <u>expensive</u> computer.

5. English is not <u>so</u> easy for me.

6. The man invited <u>my</u> sister yesterday.

B. 아래 문장에서 밑줄 친 동사를 자동사와 타동사로 구분하세요.

1. He <u>smiles</u> at me.

2. We <u>made</u> a reservation.

3. They <u>went</u> to the park in the morning.

4. I <u>found</u> the book difficult.

5. They don't <u>want</u> to take a bus.

C. 아래 문장이 몇 형식 문장인지 구분하세요.

1. The beautiful bird is singing on the tree.

2. I thought it a dog.

3. The man killed himself on Monday.

4. Seoul is the capital of Korea.

5. Could you lend me your pen?

Occupations

teacher	professor
lawyer	scientist
doctor	veterinarian
pharmacist	pilot
police officer	secretary
architect	carpenter
mechanic	photographer
painter	cook/chef
security guard	fire fighter
model	hairdresser

What do you do?

Jordan: How do you do? I am Jordan.

Logan: How do you do? My name is Logan.

Jordan: What do you do?

Logan: I am a chef. I work for a Korean Restaurant at downtown.

Jordan: Really! I like Korean food. How long have you worked for the restaurant.

Logan: I have worked for the restaurant since last year. What's your occupation?

Jordan: I am a lawyer, but I wanted to be a teacher.

Logan: Are you satisfied with your job?

Jordan: Yes, I am.

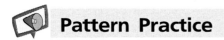

I'd like to be a _____.
My _____ is a _____.

A: What's your occupation?!
B: I am a _____.

A: Are you still a _____?
B: No, I am a _____.

Vocabulary Test

교사 _____   교수 _____

변호사 _____   과학자 _____

의사 _____   수의사 _____

약사 _____   비행기 조종사 _____

경찰관 _____   비서 _____

건축기사 _____   목수 _____

기계공 _____   주방장 _____

페인트공 _____   판매원 _____

경비원 _____   소방수 _____

모델 _____   미용사 _____

Describing A Picture

_____

_____

영어 문장의 종류(Types of sentence)

의미: 의사표현을 하는 데 있어, 말을 하는 사람이 상대방에게 혹은 제3자에게 어떤 사실이나, 상태를 자신의 의도에 따라 구분해서 문장을 선택한다.

평서문: 어떤 사실이나 상태를 평범하게 나타내는 문장
의문문: 어떤 사실이나 상태에 대해 의견 또는 대답을 요구하는 문장
명령문: 말하는 이가 자신 또는 듣는 사람에게 무엇을 시키거나 행동을 요구하는 문장
감탄문: 자신의 감정이나 느낌을 강하게 표현하는 문장

* **긍정문과 부정문**

위 문장들을 때로는 긍정문으로, 때로는 부정문으로 표현된다.

1. 평서문: 주어 + 동사의 어순으로 쓴다.

The lion runs very fast.

I am very happy.

Billy loved Jane at that time.

She bought him a bicycle.

They made her sad.

He can speak English very well.

§ 평서문의 부정문 만들기

1) be동사가 있는 평서문: be동사 뒤에 not을 붙인다.

He is a doctor.

→ He is not a doctor.

The cat is dangerous.

→ The cat is not dangerous.

2) 조동사가 있는 평서문: 조동사 뒤에 not을 붙인다.

He can speak English.

→ He can't speak English.

We will meet the mayor at the city hall.

→ We will not meet the mayor at the city hall.

3) 일반동사가 있는 평서문: 'do'동사를 일반동사 앞에 넣고 do동사 다음에 not을 붙인다.

I want to study with him.

→ I don't want to study with him.

Linda loves John.

→ Linda does not love John.

They made her sad.

→ They did not make her sad.

2. 의문문: 의문사 있는 의문문과 의문사 없는 의문문으로 구분되며, 동사 + 주어의 어순을 갖는다.

1) 의문사 없는 의문문: 주어와 동사의 어순이 동사 + 주어의 순서가 된다.

(1) be동사가 있는 평서문: be동사가 문장 앞으로 간다.

She is a famous singer.

→ Is she a famous singer?

They are angry.

→ Are they angry?

(2) 조동사가 있는 평서문: 조동사가 문장 앞으로 간다.

They can play the piano.

→ Can they play the piano.

He will write a novel.

→ Will he write a novel.

(3) 일반동사가 있는 평서문: 'do'동사를 문장 앞에 넣고, 원래 동사는 '원형'을 사용한다.

I met the woman.

→ Did I meet her?

She teaches him English.

→ Does she teach him English?

They elected the man mayor.

→ Do they elect the man mayor?

2) 의문사 있는 의문문: When, Where, Who, What, How, Why 등의 의문사가 있는 의문문으로서, 의문사는 항상 문두에 위치하며, 동사 + 주어의 어순을 유지한다.

When do you want to go there?

Where is the police station?

Who is the man over there?

What shall I do next time?

How can I help you?

Why are they so excited?

3. 명령문: 명령뿐만 아니라 청유, 정중한 부탁(간접명령)도 포함되며, 일반적으로 상대방에게 지시하는 것이기 때문에 주어 'You'가 생략되어 동사원형으로 시작된다.

Do it yourself.

Open the door, please.

Let me introduce myself.

Let me say.

* 명령문 다음에 오는 'and'는 '그러면'으로 'or'는 '그러지 않으면'으로 해석

Study hard, and you will pass the test.

Work hard, or you will be fired.

4. 감탄문: 평서문을 사용해서 감탄을 나타내기도 하고, 'how'나 'what'을 사용해서 감탄을 표현한다.

You are so beautiful!

What a nice day it is!
  (What a/an 명사 주어 동사)

How pretty it is!
  (How 형용사 주어 동사)

Exercise

A. 아래 문장의 종류를 구분하세요.

평서문, 의문문, 명령문, 감탄문

1. What a kind man he is!
2. Did you meet him yesterday?
3. Let him go.
4. Is she a teacher?
5. The program is very useful.

B. 아래 문장들을 부정문으로 만드세요.

1. My uncle was very diligent.
2. My sister watched the TV show yesterday.
3. They paint the roof white.
4. William sent Linda the jewelry box.
5. I can do it.

C. 아래 문장들을 의문문으로 만드세요.

1. He is interested in politics.
2. Susan is from America.
3. She likes to talk on the phone.
4. Birds sing in the forest.
5. She will do her best tomorrow.

Describing People

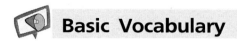

tall/short	big/small
fat/thin	straight/curly
young/old	good/bad
rich/poor	happy/unhappy
nervous	sad
miserable	upset
disappointed	frustrated
angry/mad	shocked
surprised	afraid/scared
bored	embarrassed
confused	jealous
proud	annoyed

How are you doing?

Linda: How are you today, Andrew?
    You look angry.

Andrew: I am just in a bad mood.

Linda: Why? Are you upset about something?

Andrew: Yeah, My car wouldn't start this morning.
    It was driving me crazy.

Linda: What did you do?

Andrew: I took a taxi. So, I was late at the meeting.
    There were many people waiting for me.

Linda: How about taking a break?

Andrew: Okay, This has been a long day.

Linda: See you tomorrow!

Andrew: Take care.

He is very _____.

He is _____ than me.

A: Are you _____?

B: Yes, I am _____.

A: What makes you _____.

B: _____ makes me _____.

A: When do you feel _____.

B: I am _____ when I am _____.

Vocabulary Test

비참한 _____   실망한 _____

화난 _____   짜증난 _____

좌절된 _____   충격을 받은 _____

초조한 _____   겁먹은 _____

지루한 _____   당황한 _____

질투하는 _____   혼동된 _____

불행한 _____   걱정스러운 _____

놀란 _____   만족한 _____

자랑스러운 _____   창피한 _____

두려운 _____

Describing A Picture

_____

_____

명사(Noun)

의미: 사람, 사물, 유·무형을 말하는 단어
역할: 문장에서 주어, 목적어, 보어 역할

▽ 명사의 종류

셀 수 있는 명사: 문장에서 단수, 복수 구분을 해야 한다.

보통명사, 집합명사

셀 수 없는 명사: 단수 취급을 하며, 복수형을 만들 수 없다.

물질명사, 추상명사, 고유명사

1. 보통명사: 같은 종류의 사람, 사물, 동물에 공통적으로 붙일 수 있는 명사

예) book, pen, desk, house, room, door, window, board, projector

I read a book.

He likes apples.

2. 집합명사: 사람, 또는 사물의 집합체를 나타내는 명사

1) 집합체의 단일성을 강조하면 단수취급

2) 집합체의 개별성을 강조하면 복수취급

예) family, public, audience, team, committee, faculty

His family is very large.

His family get up all early in the morning.

The committee meets once a week.

The committee express their opinions at the meeting.

3. 물질명사: 일정한 모양을 갖추지 않은 물질을 나타내는 명사

예) water, tea, coffee, paper, old, oil, milk, sugar, salt, money, sand

Milk is made into butter and cheese.

This box was made of paper.

* 물질명사의 수량 표시

a glass of water,   two glasses of water

a sheet of paper,   three sheets of paper

a bottle of beer,   two bottles of beer

a cup of coffee,   two cups of coffee

a pound of sugar,   two pounds of sugar

4. 추상명사: 눈으로 볼 수도 없고 손으로 만질 수도 없는 추상적인 무형의 명사. 원칙적으로 관사를 사용할 수 없으며, 복수형도 되지 않는다.

예) art, beauty, wisdom, truth, love, honesty, peace, news, youth, time, success, failure

Life is short and art is long.
The man was wild in his youth.

* 추상명사의 수량 표시
  a piece of information
  a piece of news
  a piece of advice

5. 고유명사: 특정한 사람, 사물, 장소, 회사에 쓰이는 고유한 이름 나타내는 명사

Hanlasan is the highest mountain in Korea.
Shakespeare is an excellent writer.
Samsung is a big company.

▽ 명사의 수

셀 수 있는 명사(보통명사, 집합명사)는 문장에서 사용될 때, 단수인지 복수인지를 확인하여 사용해야 한다. 단, 셀 수 없는 명사는 원칙적으로 단수로만 사용된다.

▽ 명사의 복수형 만들기

1. 규칙변화

1) 대부분의 단어 끝에 -s를 붙인다.

예) books, doctors, students, pens, apples, tigers, lions, sons, flowers

2) 어미가 -s, -ss, -x, -sh, -ch로 끝나면 -es를 붙인다.

예) buses, glasses, boxes, dishes, benches, peaches, brushes

3) 자음 + y로 끝나는 단어는 y를 i로 고친 뒤 -es를 붙인다.

예) ladies, cities, babies, soliloquies, duties, flies

4) 자음 + o는 -es를 붙인다.

예) potatoes, heroes, negroes, echoes

* 주의: 자음 + o라도 -s만 붙이는 경우가 있다.
    예) pianos, solos, autos, photos, memos, sopranos

5) 어미가 -f(e)로 끝나면 -f를 -ves로 고친다.

예) lives, thieves, knives, leaves, wives, wolves, shelves

* 주의: roofs, chiefs, safes, cliffs, proofs

2. 불규칙변화

1) 모음을 변화시켜 복수로 만드는 경우

예) men, feet, women, geese, teeth, mice

2) -en, -ren을 붙여 복수로 만드는 경우

예) children, oxen

3) 단수와 복수의 형태가 같은 단어

예) sheep, deer, salmon, trout, fish

Exercise

A. 아래 문장에서 명사에 밑줄을 치고, 그 종류(보통, 집합, 물질, 추상, 고유)를 쓰세요.

1. The boy wants to be a good doctor.

2. He ordered a cup of coffee.

3. The audience have to pay extra money for the concert.

4. There are many people in Seoul.

5. Honesty is very important.

B. 아래 문장에서 밑줄 친 명사가 셀 수 있는 명사인지(가산), 아닌지(불가산)를 표시 하세요.

1. There are many <u>churches</u> in the city.

2. He is a smart <u>student</u>.

3. Jane loves <u>Tom</u>.

4. She went to the <u>Busan</u>.

5. We paid much <u>money</u>.

6. <u>Glass</u> is easy to break.

7. We had much <u>snow</u> last winter.

8. The traveller wanted some <u>water</u>.

9. The <u>team</u> won the game.

10. <u>Knowledge</u> is very important.

C. 아래 문장에서 밑줄 친 부분을 바르게 고치세요. 필요하면 a/an을 첨가하세요.

1. There are many <u>potato</u> in the shop.

2. Could you lend me <u>car</u>?

3. I don't understand <u>a English</u>.

4. He come from <u>a Japan</u>.

5. <u>A milk</u> is good for health.

6. The roof is covered with <u>a snow</u>.

7. There are three <u>knife</u> on the table.

8. They took care of three <u>baby</u>.

Physical States

tired	sleepy
exhausted	hungry
thirsty	sick/ill
headache	toothache
stomachache	fever
cold	cough
infection	sunburn
chills	diarrhea
earache	rash
sore throat	runny nose

What are your symptoms?

Linda: You look tired, Andrew?

Andrew: I think I just have a cold. I didn't sleep well last three days because I had to finish my project until this morning.

Linda: What are your symptoms?

Andrew: I have a fever, sore throat and runny nose.

Linda: Did you take any medicine?

Andrew: No, I am going to see a doctor.

Linda: I think you had better hurry up. Take lots of rest and feel better soon.

Andrew: Thanks.

You look _____.
I have _____.

A: What's your symptoms?
B: I have _____.

A: When do you feel _____.
B: I am _____ when I am _____.

Vocabulary Test

피곤한 _____   졸린 _____

지친 _____   배고픈 _____

목마른 _____   아픈/병이 난 _____

두통 _____   치통 _____

복통 _____   열이 있는 _____

감기 _____   기침 _____

감염 _____   햇빛 화상 _____

오한 _____   설사 _____

귀앓이 _____   발진 _____

목이 아픔 _____   콧물 _____

Describing A Picture

_____

_____

대명사(Pronoun)

의미: 명사를 대신해서 받는 단어

역할: 문장에서 주어, 목적어, 보어 역할을 한다.

▽ **대명사의 종류: 인칭대명사, 지시대명사, 부정대명사**

§ 인칭대명사

인칭		주격	소유격	목적격	소유대명사
1인칭	단수	I	my	me	mine
	복수	we	our	us	ours
2인칭	단수	you	your	you	yours
	복수	you	your	you	yours
3인칭	단수	he	his	him	his
		she	her	her	hers
		it	its	it	
	복수	they	their	them	theirs

1. we, you, they가 일반인을 나타내는 경우가 있다. 이 때 we, you, they
   는 해석하지 않는 것이 자연스럽다.

We should keep our promise.

They say that he is honest.

You should not speak ill of others.

2. 소유대명사
소유격 + 명사 = 소유대명사

Your cell phone is new, but mine is old.

3. 재귀대명사

1) 강조 용법: 강조나 대조를 나타내기 위해 명사나 대명사 뒤에 쓰이며, 생략하여도 문법상으로 지장이 없고, 강조하는 말 뒤나 문미에 위치한다.

I myself carried the suitcase.
He did it himself.

2) 재귀적 용법: 문장의 목적어가 주어와 동일인[사물]인 경우에 쓰인다.

He killed himself.
History repeats itself.

3) 관용적 용법

He did it for himself. (혼자 힘으로)
He went there by himself. (혼자서)
The door opened of itself. (저절로(= spontaneously, automatically))

4. It의 용법

1) 앞에 나온 어구(명사, 구, 절)를 받는다.

I tried to open the box, but it was impossible.

2) 비 인칭대명사 it: 특별히 가리키는 것이 없이, 문장을 만들기 위해서 주어 자리에 쓰는 것을 말한다. 이 때 it은 시간, 계절, 날씨, 거리, 명암을 나타낸다.

What time is it now? (시간)

It is spring now. (계절)

It is fine today. (날씨)

How long does it take from here to the station? (거리)

It is dark in the room. (명암)

§ 지시대명사

1. this/these, that/those

1) 가까운 것/먼 것

This is a pen.

That is a book.

2) 전자/후자(that/this)

He keeps one dog and one cat; this is more faithful than that.

3) 명사의 반복을 피하기 위한 that/those.

The tail of a fox is longer than that of a cat.

§ 부정대명사

1. one의 용법

1) 일반적인 사람을 나타낸다. 이 때 one은 해석되지 않는다.

One should keep one's promise.
One should obey one's parents.

2) 앞에 나온 명사의 반복을 피하기 위해서 쓴다.
   a + 단수보통명사: one(같은 종류의 다른 물건)
   the/this/that + 단수보통명사: it(똑같은 바로 그 물건)

If you need a book. I will lend you one.
I bought that book, but I lost it.

2. some과 any의 용법
some은 긍정문에서, any는 의문문, 부정문, 조건문에 쓰인다.

Some of the employees work really hard.
He asked for some money, but I didn't give him any.
If you need any money, I'll lend some to you.

3. all, both, every, each

1) all은 가산명사와 쓰일 때는 복수 취급, 불가산명사와 쓰일 때는 단수 취급한다.

All of them were happy.
All the money was spent.
All were happy.

2) 부분부정: every, all, both가 부정어와 같이 쓰이면 부분부정이 된다.

He didn't eat all of the tangerines.
I did not invite all of them.
Every bird can not sing.
They don't know everything.
Both of them did not come.
I do not know both of them.

Exercise

A. 괄호 안에 알맞은 인칭대명사를 써 넣으세요.

1. This question is very difficult for (   ).

2. This pen is (   ).

3. She sent (   ) a letter.

4. (   ) work for Samsung.

5. The man asked me (   ) address.

B. 괄호 안에 알맞은 대명사를 써 넣으세요.

1. The girl showed me a red sweater, but I don't like (   ).

2. This dog is stronger than (   ).

3. They were proud of (   ) for winning the game.

4, He said the bag was (   ).

5. My mother bought me blue neck ties, and I really like (   ).

6. If you need a pen, I will give (   ) to you.

C. 아래 문장에서 밑줄 친 'it'의 쓰임을 구분하세요.

1. <u>It</u> is snowing outside.

2. How far is <u>it</u> from here to the mall.

3. Tom bought a car and he drove <u>it</u> to the school.

4. How far is <u>it</u> from here to the mall.

5. I tried to open the box, but <u>it</u> was impossible.

6. <u>It</u> is already five.

Describing Body

head	hair
forehead	eyebrow
eye	ear
nose	check
mouth	jaw
lip	tooth/teeth
tongue	neck
shoulder	chest
back	arm
elbow	waist
hip	leg
knee	foot

Where have you been yesterday?

Alice: Hi, Emma. Where have you been last Sunday?

Emma: I went to Busan. There was a film festival.

Alice: Wow! Were there many actors and actresses?

Emma: Yes. I had chance to see them. All the actresses had big eyes and small faces. Specially, foreign actresses had thin waists and long legs.

Alice: How about the actors?

Emma: All of them looked fantastic. Most of them had wide shoulders and straight noses.

Alice: I feel like going there next year. I hope to see them.

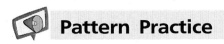

She is ——————.
She has ——————.
Her —————— is —————— than me.

I can watch TV through ——————.
I can hear the song through ——————.
I can smell the coffee through ——————.

머리 _____   머리카락 _____

앞이마 _____   눈썹 _____

눈 _____   귀 _____

코 _____   뺨 _____

입 _____   턱 _____

입술 _____   이빨 _____

혀 _____   목 _____

어깨 _____   가슴 _____

등 _____   팔 _____

팔꿈치 _____   허리 _____

엉덩이 _____   다리 _____

무릎 _____   발 _____

Describing A Picture

_____

_____

동사(Verb)

의미: 동사는 문장을 완성해 주며, '~다'로 해석한다.

역할: 주어의 행위, 동작, 상태를 나타내며, 문장을 지배하고, 시제를 나타 낸다.

1. 동사의 종류: be동사, 조동사, 일반동사

1) be동사: am, are, is로서 기본적인 뜻은 '~이다'와 '있다'로 해석되지만, 문장에 서 다양한 역할을 하므로, 특별 동사로 구분된다.

He is a student.

To be or not to be, that is a question.

There is a book on the desk.

2) 조동사: 문장에서 홀로 쓰이지 못하고, 다른 동사와 함께 쓰여 내용을 보충해 주는 역할을 한다. 대표적으로 can/could, will/would, shall/should, may/might, must, need 등이 있다.

I can speak english well.

I will do my best.

We should do study hard.

3) 일반동사: 위 두 경우를 제외하고, '~다'로 문장에서 해석되는 동사로서, 대부분의 동사가 여기에 포함된다.

> The man runs very fast.
> Anton loves Jane very much.
> They gave him a lot of money.

2. 동사의 형태

1) 현재형
주어가 3인칭 단수일 때만 원칙적으로 '-s'나 '-es'를 단어 끝에 붙인다.

> I work for the company.
> You work for the company.
> They work for the company.
> He works for the company.

* 동사가 -ch, -sh, -x, -z, -s, -o로 끝나면 '-es'를 붙인다.
watch → watches,   wash → washes,   pass → passes

* 동사가 자음 + y로 끝나면, 'y'를 'i'로 고치고 '-es'를 붙인다.
carry → carries,   study → studies,   marry → marries

2) 과거형 및 과거분사

(1) 규칙변화: 원형에 '-ed'를 붙인다.

wanted, worked, closed, noticed, visited

They worked at the plant yesterday.
Many people wanted to take a trip.
My parents visited me last Sunday.

* 1음절 어에서 모음이 하나일 경우 마지막 자음 하나를 겹쳐 쓴다.

nod - nodded - nodded	stop - stopped - stopped
beg - begged - begged	rob - robbed - begged

* 2음절에서는 둘째 음절에 accent가 있을 때만 자음을 겹친다.

omit - omitted - omitted	admit - admitted - admitted
prefer - preferred - preferred	occur - occurred - occurred

* 자음 + y인 경우는 'y'를 'i'로 고쳐서 '-ed'를 붙인다.

cry - cried - cried	try - tried - tried
study - studied - studied	carry - carried - carried

(2) 불규칙변화: 영어에는 약 350여 개 정도의 동사가 불규칙으로 변하고 있으며, 4가지 형태로 나타난다.

ABC형	see - saw - seen	break - broke - broken
ABB형	say - said - said	bring - brought - brought
ABA형	come - came - come	run - ran - run
AAA형	put - put - put	hit - hit - hit

3. 동사의 시제: 12시제

단순	과거 worked	현재 work	미래 will work
완료 have + 과거분사	had worked	have worked	will have worked
진행 be + ___ing	was working	am working	will working
완료진행 have been ___ing	had been working	have been working	will have been working

1) 현재시제

(1) 현재의 동작

Here comes the teacher.

I go to school.

(2) 현재의 상태

It is very warm today.

He lives in Korea.

(3) 현재의 습관적 동작, 습관, 직업, 성질, 능력

He is often late for school. (습관적 동작)

I get up at six every morning. (습관)

He teaches English. (직업)

She laughs too much. (성질)

She types seventy words a minute. (능력)

(4) 불변의 진리, 사실, 속담

Man is mortal. (사람은 죽게 마련이다)

The sun rises in the east.

(5) 미래의 대용: 왕래발착, 시작 등을 나타내는 동사(go, come, leave, start, begin, start, arrive, return)는 미래를 나타내는 부사(구)와 함께 현재시제로 미래시제를 대신한다.

I start for Busan tomorrow.(= will start)

He comes back next week.(= will come)

The school begins next week.(= will begin)

2) 과거시제

(1) 과거의 동작, 상태

I was born in 1976.

He met his girl friend.

(2) 과거의 습관

He would often go fishing with her.

I met him very often at the bus stop.

(3) 역사적 사실

My teacher asked me when Columbus discovered America.

3) 미래시제

자연현상, 가능(능력), 기대, 감정, 인간의 의지가 포함되지 않은 미래 등.

It will rain tomorrow.

You will be sad.

There will be no school tomorrow.

4) 현재진행

(1) 지금 진행되고 있는 동작

I am reading a novel.

It is raining now.

She's in her room studying.

(2) 미래표시 부사(구)가 왕래발착 동사의 현재 진행형과 함께 쓰이면 가까운 미래를 나타낸다.

He is leaving for America soon.

Where are you spending your next summer vacation?

* be going to + 동사원형의 용법

(1) 가까운 미래: 막 ~하려 하다.(= be about to)

I am going to write a letter.

It's going to rain.

(2) 예정/의도: ~할 작정/예정이다(사전 계획을 통해 미래에 하고자 하는 경우)

I am going to stay here for a week.

I am going to be a doctor.

(3) 미래: ~할 것이다.(= will)

It's going to storm tomorrow.

You are going to see him very often.

5) 과거진행: 과거의 어느 시점에서 진행 중인 동작을 나타낸다.

He was reading a novel when I entered the room.

6) 미래진행: 미래의 어느 시점에서 진행 중인 동작을 나타낸다.

Don't phone me between 7 and 8. We'll be having dinner then.

7) 현재완료: 현재를 기준 시점으로 하여 과거의 어느 시점에서 현재까지의 완료, 결과, 경험, 계속을 나타낸다.

(1) 완료: 현재에 있어 동작의 완료를 나타낸다. today, this year, recently, just, now, already, by this time, yet, so far 등과 같이 쓰인다.

I have not finished yet.

He has just come back home.

(2) 결과: 과거 동작에 대한 현재의 결과를 나타낸다.

He has lost his watch.(= He lost his watch and doesn't have it now)

She has bought a new car.(= She bought a new car and has it now)

She has gone to the station.(= She went to the station and is there now)

(3) 경험: 과거에서 현재까지의 동작, 상태의 경험을 나타낸다. ever, never, before, once, twice, several times, often, seldom 등과 같이 쓰인다.

I have never been to Europe.

Have you ever seen a tiger?

I have met him before.

(4) 계속: 과거에서 현재까지의 상태의 계속을 나타낸다.

She has been ill since last week.

Five years have passed since he died.

I have known him since he was a child.

8) 과거완료: 과거의 어느 때를 기준점으로 하여 그 이전에 일어난 일의 동작, 혹은 상태의 완료, 결과, 경험, 계속을 나타낸다.

(1) 완료

He had gone to bed when I came to home.

They had arrived at the house before night fell.

(2) 결과

Spring had come by the time she was well again.

(3) 계속

He had lived there for ten years when his mother died.

(4) 경험

I did not know him, for I had never seen him before.

9) 미래완료: 미래의 한 시점을 기준으로 그 때까지 일어난 동작, 혹은 상태의 완료, 결과, 계속, 경험을 나타낸다.

I shall have finished the work by the time you come. (완료)

When you awake, these fancies will have gone. (결과)

I shall have read this book three times if I read it once again. (경험)

I will have been hospital for two weeks by next Sunday. (상태계속)

10) 현재완료 진행: 과거의 어느 시점에서 시작되어 현재 시점에서도 계속되는 동작

He has been studying for ten years.
I have been reading in my study.

11) 과거완료 진행: 과거 이전의 어느 시점에 시작되어 일정 과거 시점에서도 계속되는 동작

I had been waiting for an hour when he returned.

12) 미래완료 진행: 미래의 한 시점에 진행되고 있을 동작

I shall have been reading this novel by noon.

Exercise

A. 밑줄 친 동사의 종류를 구분하세요. (be동사, 조동사, 일반동사)

1. He <u>lives</u> in Seoul.

2. I <u>believe</u> you made a mistake.

3. The man <u>became</u> a famous artist.

4. The foreigner <u>can</u> speak Korean.

5. She has <u>finished</u> her project.

6. Edward <u>was</u> a computer programer.

B. 밑줄 친 동사의 과거형을 쓰세요.

1. I <u>have</u> a lot of books.

2. She <u>writes</u> Harry Potter.

3. They <u>think</u> he is a doctor.

4. Many people <u>want</u> to see the game.

5. The player <u>hit</u> the ball.

6. I <u>read</u> a history novel.

C. 밑줄 친 동사의 시제를 구분하세요.

1. Have you ever <u>been</u> to America?

2. John is <u>staying</u> in Seoul.

3. She could not sleep well, because she <u>had had</u> much tea.

4. My brother <u>will be</u> there about 2:30.

5. The teacher <u>have been waiting</u> for his son.

Exercise Actions

stretch	bend
walk	run
hop	jump
kneel	lie down
swing	push
pull	lift
push-up	handstand
throw	kick
sit-up	pull-up
skip	somersault

Are there any sport centers around here?

Linda: Are there any sport centers around here?

Andrew: Yes. There is a sport center named 24 Hours next to the Wall-Mart.

Linda: Oh, really! I think it is a famous sport center in USA.

Andrew: Yes it is. I go to the center after work. I usually do walk and run. I can do 30 push-ups at one time.

Linda: Wow, great! I can't believe it.
I want to buy the membership card. I would like to do pull-ups everyday.

Andrew: That's good for you. I can ride you to the center.

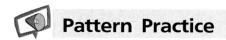

Now _____ like this.

A: Let's do twenty _____s!

B: Twenty _____s are too heavy.

A: Which exercise do you do?

B: I do _____ and _____ everyday.

쭉 펴다 _____ 구부리다 _____

걷다 _____ 달리다 _____

(깡충) 뛰다 _____ 점프하다 _____

무릎을 꿇다 _____ 눕다 _____

흔들다 _____ 밀다 _____

잡아당기다 _____ 들어 올리다 _____

팔굽혀펴기하다 _____ 물구나무서다 _____

던지다 _____ 차다 _____

윗몸일으키기하다 _____ 턱걸이하다 _____

가볍게 뛰다 _____ 재주넘기하다 _____

Describing A Picture

_____ .

_____ .

조동사(Modal Auxiliary)

의미: 조동사는 단어 특성에 따라 의미가 다양하다.

역할: 문장에서, 주가 되는 일반동사의 의미를 확대시키는 역할을 한다.

종류: can/could, will/would, shall/should, may/might. must/have to, ought, need

1. Can/Could

'Can'

1) 능력: ~할 수 있다

I can play the piano. (현재) = I am able to play the piano.

I could play the piano. (과거) = I was able to play the piano.

I shall be able to speak English. (미래)

I have been able to speak English. (현재완료)

2) 허가: ~해도 좋다

You can play here.(can = may)

Can I smoke here?

Can I go swimming?

You cannot play here. (금지) (= must not, may not)

You cannot play baseball in the garden. (금지)

3) 요청이나 제안의 표현

Can you give me a ride home?(집에 좀 태워 주시겠습니까?)
* Could you show me the way to the station?(Can보다 공손한 표현)

'Could'

1) 과거의 능력/허가

She said she could not run fast. (능력)
I could never play basketball. (능력)
I could see her yesterday. (허가)
He could go out for an hour. (허가)

2) 현재의 가능성

This could be the chance you have been looking for.
You could be right, but I don't think you are.
We could go on a picnic.

2. May/Might

'May'

1) 허가: ~해도 좋다, ~할 수 있다(= be allowed to ~, be permitted to ~)

You may go there. ↔ You may not go there.
May I use your phone?

2) 현실적 가능성(능력): ~할 수도 있다(= can)

He may know it. ↔ He may not know it. (그는 아마 모를 것이다)
Anyone may see the difference between the two.

3) 추측: ~일지 모른다.

He may be ill. (현재)
He may have been ill. (과거)

4) 기원문

May you be happy!
May he rest in peace!

'Might'

1) may의 과거 시제

He said that it might rain. (추측)

I asked if I might come in. (허가)

I thought one might see that at a glance. (가능)

We worked hard so that we might succeed. (목적)

However hard he might try, he never succeeded. (양보)

2) 가정법에서 가능성

If he had been in New York, he might have been ill.

You might at least apologize.

I might have been a rich.

3. Must/Have to

'Must'

1) 필요/의무: ~해야 한다

You must do as you are told.(= have to)

You must put on these clothes.(= have to)

2) 강한 추측: ~임에 틀림없다, 반드시 ~일 것이다

He must be ill. ↔ He cannot be ill. (현재)
He must have been ill. ↔ He cannot have been ill. (과거)

3) 필연/불가피: 반드시 ~하다

We must all die sometime.
Sooner or later, death must come to us all!

'Have to'

1) 필요/의무: must와 일반적으로 같은 뜻이나, 필요성이나 긴급함의 의미가 must 보다 약하다.

I'm looking for Susie. I have to talk to her about our lunch date
tomorrow.

2) have got to: 'have to'가 공식적, 비공식적 표현에 두루 쓰이는 반면에, 'have got to'는 비공식적 구어표현에만 쓰인다.

I have to go now. = I have got to now. = I've gotta go now.
= I gotta go now.

4. Will/Shall

1) 화자(speaker)의 의지

He shall die.(= I will kill him)

You shall have it.(= I will give it to you)

My son shall bring the money to you.

> (= I will let my son bring the money to you)

2) 청자(hearer)의 의지

Shall my daughter go first?

> (= Do you want me to let my daughter go first?)

Shall he come again?

> (= Will you let him come again?)

Will you lend me the book?

3) 주어의 의지: 인칭에 관계없이 모두 will을 써서, 의지/고집/주장을 나타낸다.

I will do as I like.

Do what you will.

I shall be very glad if you will help me.

She said, "I will leave here."

5. Would

1) 단순/의지 미래의 과거형

He said that he would pay back.

2) will 보다 공손한 표현이나 초대, 권유를 나타낸다.

Would you mind opening the door? (공손한 표현)
Would you like some coffee? (권유)

3) 과거의 습관적 행동

He would sit for hours without saying a word. (습관적 행동)
He would often come back drunk, and beat his wife. (습관적 행동)

4) 과거의 추측

He would be about twenty when he crossed the Pacific on a yacht
alone.

5) 과거의 강한 거절, 고집

I offered him money, but he would not accept it.
She would not listen to me, whatever I might say.

6) 가능성(= could)

The hall would seat 1,000 people.

6. Should

1) 의무/당연: 이 때 'should'는 'must'보다 '의무/당연'의 의미가 약해서 '권고' 또는 '타당함'의 의미를 가지며, had better와 같은 뜻으로 쓰이지만, 그 강도가 'had better'보다 약하다.

Children should obey their parents.(should = ought to)
The young should respect the old.(should = ought to)

2) 가능성/추측(should = ought to)

It should be fine tomorrow.
He should arrive by the 8:00 train.
They should be there by now, I think.

* 주장/명령/요구/제안/충고/권고/결정의 동사 뒤에 이어지는 절에서 should가 쓰인다.
이때 should는 해석되지 않으며, 생략되어 쓰이는 것이 일반적이다.

insist/order, command/desire, require, request, demand, ask/propose, suggest/advise/recommend/decide, determine

I insist that he (should) be sent there.

I propose that the matter (should) be put to the vote at once.

7. Ought to

의무/당연(ought to = should)

He ought to obey his parents.

You ought to start at once.

I told him that he ought to look for her.(= must)

8. Need

1) 긍정문에서 항상 본동사로 쓰이며, 명사나 to부정사를 목적어로 가진다.

He needs to go there.

He needs some money.

He needed to go there.

2) 부정문과 의문문에서 조동사나 본동사로 쓰인다.

He doesn't need to go there. (본동사)

Does he need to go there? (본동사)

He need not go there. (조동사)

He didn't need to go there. (본동사의 과거시제)

Did he need to go there? (본동사의 과거시제)

§ 다음의 동사들은 문장에서 본래의 뜻은 나타내지 못하고, 문장에서 기능으로만 역할을 할 때가 있으며, 마치 조동사의 역할을 하는 것 같다.

'Do'

1) 강조의 조동사: 본동사 앞에 놓여 본동사를 강조한다.

I do think you ought to go there.
I do wish children weren't so noisy.

2) 의문문과 부정문에서

Do you know him?
You did not finish it.

'Have'

완료구문을 만들기 위해 쓰인다.

I have finished the work already.
A new highway has been built.

'Be'

진행형이나 수동태 구문에서 조동사로 쓰인다.

The president is delivering a speech.

Two large pizzas were delivered.

Exercise

A. 아래 문장에서 알맞은 것을 고르세요.

1. Eliot (could, must) be on vacation this week.

2. He (might, have to) meet me at the theater.

3. The boy (can, could) attend the English class in the evening.

4. You (could, should) do obey your parents.

5. They insist that he (should, will) be sent there.

6. (May, Must) I borrow your pen?

7. (Can, Will) I ask you a question?

8. (May, Shall) we dance?

9. (Would, Should) you help me?

10. (Could, May) you be quite, please.

Sports

jogging	running
walking	roller skating
cycling	skateboarding
bowling	skydiving
golf	tennis
squash	racquetball
ping pong	handball
baseball	softball
football/soccer	hockey
basketball	volleyball

What do you do in your free time?

Bill: What do you do in your free time?

Andrew: I usually watch TV.
　　　Specially, I like to watch a golf game.

Bill: Do you have any plans for this weekend?
　　It will be a beautiful day.

Andrew: I don't have any plans for this weekend.

Bill: Good. Let's go to see a baseball game at Chamsil Stadium? It will
　　be a big game.

Andrew: That's good. The game will be exciting.
　　　I need a change.

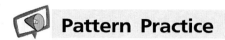 **Pattern Practice**

Individual sports/Team sports

Indoor sports/Outdoor sports

A: Which sports do you like to play?
B: I like to play ——————.

A: What are the popular sports in your country?
B: I think they are ——————.

Vocabulary Test

조깅 _____

걷기 _____

자전거타기 _____

볼링 _____

골프 _____

스쿼시 _____

탁구 _____

야구 _____

축구 _____

농구 _____

달리기 _____

롤러스케팅 _____

스케이트보딩 _____

스카이다이빙 _____

테니스 _____

라켓볼 _____

핸드볼 _____

소프트볼 _____

하키 _____

배구 _____

Describing A Picture

_____

_____

관사(Article)

의미: 형용사에 포함되어 있으며, 그 뜻은 기본적으로 '하나의'(a/an) 혹은 '그'(the)로 나타낸다.

역할: 항상 명사 앞에 쓰이며, 그 명사를 한정한다.

종류: 부정관사 'a/an'과 정관사 'the'가 있다.

1. 부정관사 'a/an'

1) one의 약한 뜻으로 보통 해석하지 않는다.

She is an honest girl.

He is a smart boy.

2) '하나'(one의 강한 뜻)

He will finish it in a day or two.

Rome was not built in a day.

Please give me an apple.

3) the same

They are of an age.

Birds of a feather flock together.

of a size(크기가 같은)/of a mind(마음이 맞는)/of a humor(기질이 같은)

4) per(~에, ~마다)

We take three meals a day.
I write to her once a month.
This cloth is 1000 won a yard.

5) any(어떤 ~라도, 모든): 대표단수

A dog is a faithful animal.
A horse is a useful animal.

6) a certain(어떤)의 뜻

A Mr. Jones came to see you.

7) some(어느 정도, 약간)의 뜻

He was speechless for a time. (얼마 동안, 당분간)
Oil paintings look better at a distance. (거리를 두고)

2. 정관사 'the'

1) 앞에 나온 명사를 반복할 경우

The other day I met a boy. The boy was flying a kite.

He lost a purse, and the purse was found in the garbage.

2) 전후관계로 명백히 알 수 있는 경우

Open the door, please.

The post office is near the school.

3) 수식어귀(형용사구, 형용사절)에 의해서 뒤에서 한정될 때: 특정한 것

The principal of our school is Mr. Han.

The water of this well is not good to drink.

She is the girl whom I met yesterday.

4) 유일한 것

The moon is the satellite of the earth.

He traveled around the world.

5) 종족 전체를 나타낼 때(대표단수)

The dog is a faithful animal.

The horse is a useful animal.

6) 서수, 최상급, only, same 앞에서 쓰인다.

I took the first train.

He is the tallest boy in our class.

You are the only student who can do it.

I have the same sharp-pencil as you have.

7) 시간, 수량의 단위를 나타낼 때: by + the + 명사(~로, ~당)

He is paid by the day(week, month).

She rented the apartment by the month.

Sugar is sold by the pound.

Cloth is sold by the yard.

8) 신체의 일부분을 표시할 때

catch, take, hold + 사람(목적격) + by the 신체일부

He caught me by the neck.[by the arm/by the hand]

9) 강, 바다, 해협 등의 이름 앞에

the Thames, the Han River/the Pacific, the Atlantic, the East Sea
/the English Channel, the Straits of Korea, the Magellan
Strait.

10) 산맥, 군도, 반도의 이름 앞에

the Alps, the Rocky Mountains/the Philippines, the West Indies
/the Korean Peninsula

3. 관사의 생략

1) 일반적 의미의 불가산명사 및 복수명사 앞에는 관사를 쓰지 않는다.

Water must be pure if it is to be drunk.

Museums are closed on Monday.

2) 호격일 경우

Waiter, give me a cup of coffee.

Father, may I go out?

3) 가족관계일 경우

Mother goes to market in the afternoon.

Father is out, but mother is in.

4) 관직, 신분을 나타내는 말이 동격 또는 보어로 쓰일 때

Elizabeth I, Queen of England, was a great monarch.

They elected him mayor of the city.

He was appointed principal.

5) 명사(건물)가 본래의 목적으로 사용될 때

She goes to church every Sunday.

She goes to the church to see her.

He goes to school every day.

He goes to the school to play baseball.

The man went to prison. (투옥되다)

His wife went to the prison to see him.

6) 식사, 운동, 학과, 질병 이름 앞에

We eat breakfast at seven.

He came immediately after dinner.

He plays tennis every Sunday.

He specializes in mathematics.

He died of cancer.

7) 교통수단

by plane[air](= on a plane)/by train(= on a train)/by ship(= on a ship)
/by car(= in a car)/by bus(= on a bus)/by sea(해로로)
/on horseback, by coach(마차로)/on foot

8) 통신수단

by telephone/by wireless(무선으로)/by radio(무전으로)/by telegram(전보로)

Exercise

A. 밑줄 친 단어 앞에 관사가 필요하면 써 넣으세요.

1. Dog is <u>faithful</u> animal.

2. I need to <u>teacher</u> to help me.

3. I think she is <u>music</u> dancer.

4. <u>Water</u> is very important.

5. One of my friends lives in <u>Seoul</u>.

6. We should know <u>life</u> is not so long.

B. 밑줄 친 부정관사의 의미를 보기에서 찾아 쓰세요.

보기) one, per, some, a certain

1. They talked about <u>a</u> movie. _____

2. There is <u>an</u> apple on the table. _____

3. My son usually drink two glasses of milk <u>a</u> day. _____

4. You had better take a rest for <u>a</u> day or two. _____

5. My mother will stay here for <u>a</u> time. _____

C. 빈 칸에 알맞은 관사를 써 넣으세요.

1. (　　　　　) caw is a useful animal

2. I don't have (　　　　) driver's license.

3. Yesterday, I bought a USB, but I lost (　　　　) USB.

4. Please, open (　　　　) door.

5. (　　　　) sun rises in the east.

6. He caught me by (　　　　) hand.

Sports 105

Fruits & Vegetables

 **Basic Vocabulary**

apple	banana	coconut
kiwi	peach	pear
plum	mango	orange
lemon	pineapple	grapes
strawberries	cantaloup	honeydew
watermelon		

cabbage	celery	lettuce
corn	broccoli	asparagus
spinach	carrot	tomato
potato	sweet potato	radish
onion	green onion	cucumber
mushroom		

When is the Farmer's Market open?

Linda: When is the Farmer's Market open?

Andrew: It is open every Saturday near downtown.

Linda: How about going there this Saturday?
We need apples, cantaloupes, celeries, potatoes and mushrooms.
Do they sell fresh fruits and vegetables?

Andrew: Yes, I heard about that. But, the price of them are not so cheap.

Linda: I think there are also some special events at the market.

Andrew: What kinds of events?

Linda: A group concert and a magic show.

Andrew: There will be many people at the market.

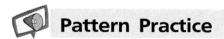

My favorite fruit is _____?

The _____ is a basis vegetables for breakfast.

A: This _____ are delicious?

Where did you buy it?

B: I bought the _____ at E-mart.

A: Which vegetables do you like?

B: I really like _____.

Vocabulary Test

사과 _____ 바나나 _____ 코코넛 _____

키위 _____ 복숭아 _____ 배 _____

자두 _____ 망고 _____ 오렌지 _____

레몬 _____ 파인애플 _____ 포도 _____

딸기 _____ 머스크멜론 _____ 멜론 _____

수박 _____

양배추 _____ 셀러리 _____ 양상추 _____

옥수수 _____ 브로콜리 _____ 버섯 _____

시금치 _____ 당근 _____ 토마토 _____

감자 _____ 고구마 _____ 무 _____

양파 _____ 파 _____ 오이 _____

아스파라가스 _____

Describing A Picture

_____

_____

형용사(Adjective)

의미: 성질이나 상태를 나타냄.

역할: 문장에서 명사를 바로 꾸며주거나, 명사를 보충 설명해 주는 역할을
한다.

1. 형용사의 용법

1) 한정용법: 형용사가 명사의 앞 또는 뒤에서 직접 수식하는 것을 말한다.

She is a smart student.

I found an empty box.

2) 서술용법: 형용사가 주어나 목적어를 풀이해 주는 역할을 한다.
즉, 주격보어나 목적격보어로 쓰인다.

The baby is very pretty.

I found him honest.

2. 형용사의 위치

1) 형용사의 어순: 여러 개의 형용사가 올 경우는 대개 다음의 순서를 따른다.
한정사 + 수량(서수/기수) + 대소 + 성상 + 색 + 신구/노소 + 재료/소속/기원

Look at the two large fine old stone houses.

She is a tall thin French lady.

  * 한정사: 소유격, 관사, 대명형용사, 부정형용사(some, any, no, little, few, etc.)

2) '-thing', '-body'를 수식하는 형용사는 뒤에서 수식한다.

Please give me something cold to drink.

He is a somebody important.

3. 형용사의 명사 표현

1) the + 형용사: 복수보통명사

The rich stayed the famous hotel.

예) the rich = rich people   the poor = poor people
    the young = young people   the wise = wise people

2) the + 형용사: 추상명사

The woman has an eye the beautiful.

예) the true = truth/the good = good(善)
    /the beautiful = beauty(美)

4. 수사

1) 기수: one, hundred, thousand, million, billion

* dozen, score, hundred, thousand, million 은 복수수사 다음에 쓰여도 's'를 쓰지 않는다.
  예) three score, two hundred, five million

* 막연히 많은 숫자를 나타낼 때는 복수형을 쓴다.
  예) dozens of people   scores of students   hundreds of people
        thousands of people   millions of people

2) 서수: first, second, third, fifth, eighth, ninth, tenth.

3) 분수: 분자는 기수로 분모는 서수로 읽으며, 분자를 먼저 읽고 분모를 읽으며, 분자가 복수일 때는 분모의 서수를 복수형(-s)으로 해주어야 한다.

예) ½: a half or one half, ⅓: one third or a third, ⅔: two thirds
    ¼: one fourth or a quarter,
    134/200: one hundred (and) thirty four over two hundred

4) 소수: 소수점은 point로 읽고, 소수점 뒤의 숫자는 하나씩 따로 읽는다.

1.23: one point two three
0.23: zero point two three
13.704: thirteen point seven zero four

5) 배 수사: once, twice, three times, ten times

This is as large as that.

He has twice the number of my books.

This is three times as large as that.

This is three times the size of that.

6) 연도 등

1991: nineteen ninety-one

1990's: nineteen nineties

387-6077: three eight seven six o double seven

5. 수량형용사

1) Many(수): 많은, + 셀 수 있는 명사

Many students have repeated the same mistakes.

* as many: 동수의

He made ten mistakes in as many lines.

There were five accidents in as many days.

2) Much(양): 많은, + 셀 수 없는 명사

I have much money.

* as much: 동량의

I thought as much.(그 만큼은, 그 정도는)

He drank two bottles of beer and as much wine.

3) Few(수): 조금, + 셀 수 있는 명사
few(거의 없는: 부정), a few(조금 있는: 긍정)

He has few friends.

He has a few friends.

4) Little(양): 조금, + 셀 수 없는 명사
little(거의 없는: 부정), a little(조금 있는: 긍정)

I have little money with me.

I have a little money with me.

Exercise

A. 밑줄 친 형용사가 꾸며주는 명사를 고르세요.

1. I was late at the meeting because of <u>heavy</u> traffic.

2. Something <u>spicy</u> was put into her soup.

3. There is a ugly <u>broken</u> car on the street.

4. I met somebody <u>famous</u> at the mall.

5. My <u>favorite</u> sport is baseball.

B. 밑줄 친 형용사가 설명해 주고 있는 단어(명사 또는 대명사) 또는 구를 고르세요.

1. The city is <u>fantastic</u>.

2. My mother always made me <u>happy</u>.

3. I know he is very <u>smart</u>.

4. I think they believed him <u>honest</u>.

C. 문장에 알맞은 것을 고르세요.

1. I have (a few, a little) breakfast in the morning.

2. He spent (many, much) days doing his project.

3. There is (many, much) snow in this winter.

4. How (many, much) pictures did you take in USA.

5. I don't have (a few, a little) knowledge about it.

6. The man want to get (a few, a little) notebooks.

Everyday Activities

get up

brush my teeth

take a show

make breakfast

clean the house

wash the dishes

do the laundry

exercise

return home

get dressed

shave

make the bed

have breakfast

vacuum

drive a car

watch TV

make a phone call

go to bed

What do you do in the morning?

Charles: What do you do in the morning?

Andrew: I usually make breakfast and wash the dishes.

Charles: How about in the afternoon?

Andrew: I don't have any plans.

Charles: Me, too. Shall we take a walk at the civic park. It is beautiful outside.

Andrew: Good! I need to exercise.

Charles: See you at 12 at the park.

Andrew: O.K. See you there.

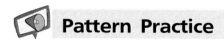 **Pattern Practice**

I _____ before having breakfast.

I _____ after having lunch.

A: What do you do in the morning?

B: I _____ in the morning.

A: Wat are you doing?

B: I am _____.

Vocabulary Test

일어나다 _____   옷을 입다 _____

이빨을 닦다 _____   면도하다 _____

샤워하다 _____   잠자리 정돈하다 _____

아침밥을 만들다 _____   아침밥을 먹다 _____

집을 청소하다 _____   공기청소하다 _____

설거지하다 _____   운전하다 _____

세탁하다 _____   TV를 보다 _____

운동하다 _____   전화 걸다 _____

집에 돌아오다 _____   잠자리에 들다 _____

_____.

_____.

부사(Adverb)

의미: 성질, 상태, 동작, 문장 등의 의미를 보다 분명하게 함.

역할: 문장에서 동사, 형용사, 부사 또는 문장 전체를 수식한다.

시간, 장소, 방법, 정도, 빈도 등을 나타낸다.

1. 부사의 기능

1) 동사 수식

He speaks English well.

He did not die happily.

2) 형용사 수식

She is very clever.

This is too expensive.

3) 부사 수식

They lived very happily.

4) 문장 전체 수식

Happily he did not die.

Unfortunately he died.

Probably he will succeed this time.

2. 부사 형태

1) 형용사에다가 '-ly'를 붙인다.

slow - slowly   careful - carefully   glad - gladly

2) 형용사와 같은 형태의 부사: early, long, hard, enough, fast, pretty, late, high 등은 형용사와 부사의 형태가 같다.

The early bird catches the worm.

I get up early in the morning.

She wrote a long letter to her teacher.

He was long ill.

He has money enough for his trip.

She is old enough to love.

He is fast runner.

He eats fast.

3) 형용사와 같은 형태의 부사와 -ly형의 부사가 뜻이 서로 다른 경우가 있다.

It is hard to understand.(어려운)

He studies hard.(열심히)

He hardly studies.(거의 않는)

I was late for school today.

The doctor came too late.

I haven't seen him lately.

She is pretty. (귀여운)

He is pretty well now. (상당히, 꽤)

She is prettily dressed. (예쁘게)

Mt. Baegdu is very high.

The cat can jump high.

It is a highly interesting movie. (굉장히)

2. 부사의 위치

1) 빈도부사의 위치

종류: always, never, often, sometimes, seldom, rarely, scarcely, regularly, ever, usually

위치: 빈도부사 + 일반동사

be동사 + 빈도부사

조동사 + 빈도부사 + 본동사

He is always at home.

I have never been to England.

I can scarcely understand his words.

It seldom snows in Busan.

* 여러 개의 낱말로 이루어진 구 형태의 빈도부사는 문미나 문두에 위치한다.

now and then, from time to time, on occasion, all the time, twice a week, now and again, every two days

I go to the language school every two days.

2) 장소 + 방법 + 시간
시간부사어구: 작은 단위 + 큰 단위
장소부사어구: 좁은 장소 + 넓은 장소
일반부사(구): 짧은 부사(구) + 긴 부사(구)

I'll visit you at seven o'clock next Sunday.
We arrived safely at the station.
He arrived there safely yesterday.
We lived there happily before.
I met him at the station at five o'clock.

3. 주의해야 할 부사의 용법

1) enough: 일반적으로 부사가 형용사, 부사를 수식할 때는 형용사 앞에 놓이는 것이 원칙이지만, enough는 수식하는 말 뒤에 놓인다.

He does not work enough.
He is rich enough to buy the Volvo.

2) only: 관계가 가장 밀접한 것과 가까이 두는 것이 원칙이다.

Only I can see him in the room.

I can only see him in the room.

I can see only him in the room.

I can see him only in the room.

3) already와 yet

already는 긍정문에 사용: 이미, 벌써

Linda has already gone to bed.

Has the bell rung already?

yet은 의문문, 부정문에 사용

Has the bell rung yet? (벌써, 이미)

The work is not yet finished. (아직)

* 긍정문에 yet가 사용되면: 아직, 여전히

She is talking yet.

4) ago와 before

ago: 현재를 기준으로 하여 '지금부터 ~전'의 뜻. 항상 과거시제에 사용

before: 과거를 기준으로 하여 '그때부터 ~전'의 뜻. 주로 과거완료에 사용

My father died ten years ago.

I had received a letter three days (ago, before).

When I met him two years ago, he said his son had died five years before.

5) 유도부사 there: 문두에서 동사를 이끄는 역할을 한다.

There is a book.

There is no one there.

There seems to have been a fire.

Exercise

A. 밑줄 친 부사가 꾸며주는 것을 찾으세요.

1. The doctor talks <u>very</u> fast.

2. <u>Unfortunately</u>, he was absent.

3. He is old <u>enough</u> to take a trip by himself.

4. I slept <u>deeply</u> yesterday.

5. My son learns language <u>quickly</u>.

B. 주어진 부사(구)를 문장에 알맞게 써 넣으세요.

1. She gets up early in the morning. (usually)

2. He is rich to buy the car. (enough)

3. Tom can speak English. (well)

4. I used to go shipping with my husband. (all the time)

5. I am happy to meet you. (really)

C. 밑줄 친 단어의 뜻을 쓰세요.

1. The bus arrived ten minutes <u>late</u>.

2. I haven't seen him <u>lately</u>.

3. The man is working <u>hard</u>.

4. He <u>hardly</u> ever go to church.

5. The cat can jump <u>high</u>.

6. It is a <u>highly</u> interesting movie.

Place around town

convenience store	bank
bakery	cafeteria
clinic/hospital	hotel
day care center	cleaners
department	drug store/pharmacy
concert hall	museum
movie theater	library
gas station	grocery store
laundromat	parking lot
post office	police station
restaurant	train station

Where are you going?

Linda: Hi, how are you today?

Andrew: Pretty good. Where are you going?

Linda: I am going to a department store. There is a big sale at the store. Do you want to join me.

Andrew: I really want to, but I am going to the city library. I have to read a special book.

Linda: Is the library open today? It's Sunday!

Andrew: Yes, it is. The cafeteria next to the library is also open today. I will have lunch at the cafeteria. Enjoy your shopping!

Linda: See you tomorrow.

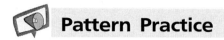

Pattern Practice

Is there a/an _____ nearby?

There is a/an _____ around the school.

A: Where are you going?

B: I am going to the _____.

A: Where is the _____?

B: It is next to the _____.

Vocabulary Test

편의점 _____   은행 _____

식당 _____   셀프서비스 식당 _____

병(의)원 _____   제과점 _____

놀이방 _____   세탁소 _____

백화점 _____   약국 _____

연주 홀 _____   박물관 _____

영화관 _____   도서관 _____

주유소 _____   식품점 _____

빨래방 _____   주차장 _____

우체국 _____   경찰서 _____

호텔 _____   기차역 _____

Describing A Picture

_____

_____

접속사(Conjunction)

역할: 단어와 단어, 구와 구, 절과 절을 연결한다.

1. 등위접속사

1) 완전등위접속사: 완전히 대등한 단문이나 구를 연결시키는 접속사를 말한다.

(1) 'and'
- 단일 개념을 나타낸다.

Time and tide wait(s) for no man.
Slow and steady wins the race.
Bread and butter is my favorite breakfast.

- 부정사 대신에 쓰는 경우: go, come, try, send, run, mind, write 등의 다음에 오는 and는 to 부정사의 대용으로 쓰여 '목적(~하기 위해서)'의 의미를 가진다.

Come and see me.(= Come to see me)
Try and use plain words.(= Try to use plain words)

- 명령문 + and: ~하라, 그러면

Work hard, and you will succeed.
Push the button, and the door will open.

(2) 'but'
Excuse me, but what is your name?

(3) 'or'
- or: 말하자면, 즉(= that is, that is to say)
I weigh 110 pounds or about 50 kilograms.

- 명령문 + or = unless, if ~ not(~하라, 그렇지 않으면)
Work hard, or you will fail.(= Unless you work hard, you will fail.)

2) 등위접속사: 거의 대등한 두 구나 단문을 연결시키는 접속사를 말한다.

(1) 'for': comma 뒤에 쓰여서 추가적 이유/원인을 설명한다.
She does not go out in winter, for she feels the cold a great deal.
She was sleeping, for she worked all day.

(2) 'so' 그래서, ~이므로
I'm feeling a bit under the weather today, so can you come some other
day?

3) 등위 상관접속사

Either you or I am to blame. (A 또는 B 둘 중의 하나)

He can neither ski nor swim. (A와 B 둘 다 아닌)

Both butter and cheese are nutritious foods. (A와 B 둘 다)

* not only A but (also) B = B as well as A(A뿐만 아니라 B 역시)

Not only you but also I was wrong. = You as well as I are wrong.

Not money but wisdom is what I want. (A가 아니고 B인)

2. 종속접속사

1) 명사절을 이끄는 접속사

(1) 'That': 주로 단정적인 내용을 이끈다.

   - 주절, 목적절, 주격보어절을 이끈다.

That he has gone is certain. (주절)

I think it a pity that you didn't try harder. (목적절)

The trouble is that we are short of money. (주격보어절)

(2) 'whether': '~인지 어떤지(아닌지)'의 의미로 양자택일을 요하는 문장을 이끈다.

   - 주절을 유도

It is very doubtful whether he will consent (or not). (진주어절)

Whether he is wise or stupid is not important problem.

- 목적절을 유도(whether = if)

I wonder whether the news is true.

I don't know whether he is at home or at the office.

I am not sure whether he will pass the final test (or not).

2) 부사절을 이끄는 접속사

- 시간의 부사절을 이끄는 접속사

(1) 'when/as/whenever'

When her husband had an accident, she was coming home for work.

Give her this letter when she comes. (~할 때에, ~하면(= if))

They were about to start fighting when their father intervened. (바로 그때)

He came up as she was speaking. (~할 때(= when))

Whenever I felt lonely, I used to visit his house. (~할 때는 언제나)

(2) 'until'

~할 때까지

We stayed there until we finished our work.

(3) 'before'

긍정문 + before: ~해서야(지나서야) 비로소 ~하다

It will be long before he notices it.(한참 지나서야 그가 알게 될 것이다)

It was five years before I met Jane again.(5년이 지나서야 비로소 Jane을 다시 만났다)

(4) 'after'

I'll go after I finish my work.

(5) 'since': ~이후로, ~이래로

Five years have passed since his father died.

He came to New York two years ago and has lived here ever since.

– 이유/원인의 부사절을 이끄는 접속사

(1) 'because': 직접적인 이유/원인을 나타낸다.

He could finish the work because he worked hard.

I did not go because I wanted to.(내가 원해서 간 것은 아니었다)

(2) 'since': because보다 의미가 약하며, 간접적인 이유/원인을 나타낸다.

Since no one agrees to my proposal, I will give it up.

(3) 'for': because보다 의미가 약하며, comma 뒤에 쓰여서 추가[보충]적 이유/원인을 설명한다.

She was sleeping, for she worked all day.(for=because)

(4) 'as': since보다 의미가 약하며, 간접적인 이유/원인을 나타낸다.

As it was cold yesterday, I stayed home all day.

– 목적의 부사절을 이끄는 접속사

(so) that ~ may[can] = in order that ~ may[can]: ~하기 위하여

He worked hard so that he might succeed.

I packed her some food (so) that he wouldn't get hungry.

– 결과의 부사절을 이끄는 접속사

so + 형용사/부사 + that ~/such + a(an) + 형용사 + 명사 + that ~: 너무 ~해서 ~하다

It was so hot that we went swimming.

It was such a nice weather that we went out for a walk.

– 양보의 부사절을 이끄는 접속사

(1) though = although = even though

Though he is poor, he is happy.[although 보다는 구어적인 의미를 가짐]

Even though I don't love her, I have to marry her.(비록 ~라 하더라도)

(2) if/even if

If he is poor, he is a nice guy.

Even if we are not rich, we have good friends.

– 장소의 부사절을 이끄는 접속사(where/wherever)

God knows where he comes from.

Go wherever you want to go.

– 양태의 부사절을 이끄는 접속사

(1) as: ~처럼, ~대로

Do in Rome as the Romans do.

As you treat me, so will I treat you.

(2) as if/as though: 마치 ~처럼

He talks as if he knew everything.

– 조건을 이끄는 접속사(if)

If it's cold tomorrow, I will stay at home.

Exercise

A. 문장에서 접속사가 연결하고 있는 것에 밑줄 치세요.

1. I want to buy apples and tomatoes at the shop.

2. We should take this bus or wait for next one.

3. Tom lost his wallet, but his wife found it at the park.

4. To be or not to be, that is a question.

B. 빈칸에 알맞은 단어를 써 넣으세요.

1. (   ) she (   ) I were satisfied with the result.

2. (   ) John or Jane will be a first player.

C. 접속사가 이끄는 절에 밑줄을 치세요.

1. He told me that he couldn't take the position.

2. My wife asked if I wanted to have lunch at home.

3. Mike thought that I had made a mistake.

4. I wonder weather Linda told a lie.

5. That she is honest is clear.

Weather & Seasons

winter	spring
summer	autumn/fall

warm	cool
cold	freezing
sunny	clear
cloudy	windy
foggy	humid
raining	hailing
snowing	

lighting	tornado
snowstorm	thunderstorm
typhoon	

fahrenheit	centigrade

Winter is a ski season!

Linda: What's the weather forecast?

Andrew: It will be sunny tomorrow.

Linda: That's great! Let's go skiing tomorrow.

Andrew: The road condition will be good to drive.

Linda: There are a lot of snow at the mountain.

Andrew: It will be cold at the mountain. We have to take extra winter parkers.

Linda: That's good idea. Mountains are usually much colder than downtown.

Andrew: It will be exciting tomorrow.

Linda: Winter is a ski season. I have wanted to see lots of snow this winter.

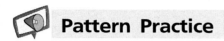 **Pattern Practice**

My favorite season is _____ because _____.
It will be _____ tomorrow.

A: How is the weather?
B: It is _____.

A: What's the temperature?
B: It is ten degrees _____.

겨울 _____   봄 _____

여름 _____   가을 _____

따듯한 _____   시원한 _____

추운 _____   매우 추운 _____

화창한 _____   맑은 _____

구름 낀 _____   바람이 있는 _____

안개 낀 _____   습한 _____

비가 오는 _____   우박이 내리는 _____

눈이 오는 _____

번개 _____   토네이도 _____

눈보라 _____   천둥 _____

태풍 _____

화씨 _____   섭씨 _____

Describing A Picture

_____.

_____.

전치사(Preposition)

의미: 다른 품사 단어, 구 절 앞에 놓여, 그 의미를 나타냄.

1. 전치사의 목적어

전치사 뒤에 나오는 단어, 구, 절 등을 전치사의 목적어라 한다. 전치사의 목적어로는 명사, 대명사, 형용사, 과거분사, 부사, 동명사, 부정사, 구, 절이 올 수 있다.

1) 명사, 대명사

He goes to school by bus.

He lives with Tom.

Let's play with them.

I bought a pencil for him.

* 전치사의 목적어로 대명사가 올 때는 반드시 목적격을 써주어야 한다.

2) 형용사, 과거분사, 부사

Things went from bad to worse.

You should not take your parent's sacrifice for granted.

He returned from abroad.

It is far from here.

3) 동명사, 부정사

He is fond of driving in the country.

He is afraid of going alone.

There is nothing but to wait.

I was about to leave.

4) 구

He appeared from behind the tree.

He read the book till late at night.

5) 절

From where I was sitting I could not see them.

He will not work except when he is pleased.

2. 전치사의 종류

1) 장소를 나타내는 전치사

at: 비교적 좁은 장소에 사용.

in: 넓은 장소에 사용.

I live at Chongro in Seoul.

He is standing at the door.

I was staying at a hotel in New York.

on: 접촉하여 '위에'   above: 막연한 '위로'(보다 높이)

beneath: 접촉하여 '아래에'   below: 막연한 '아래로'(보다 아래로)

over: 수직으로 바로 '위에'   up: 밑에서 '위(쪽으)로'

under: 수직으로 바로 '아래에'   down: 위에서 '아래(쪽으)로'

There is a vase on the table.

The ice gave way beneath our feet.

The moon has risen above the horizon.

The sun has just sunk below the horizon.

A jet plane flew over the city.

He was lying under the tree.

They went up and down the street.

We sailed down the river.

between: 둘 사이에

among: 셋 이상 사이에

There is a river between the two villages.

Many birds are singing among the trees.

behind: ~의 뒤에   Who is the man behind the tree?

after: 뒤를 쫓아   The dog ran after the rabbit.

in: ~의 안에   I study in this room.

into: ~의 안으로   He came into the room.

out of: ~의 밖으로   He came out of the room.

across: ~을 가로질러, ~을 횡단하여

through: ~을 통과하여

along: ~에 연하여, ~을 따라서

    He came across the street.

    The train passed through the tunnel.

    We walked along the river.

round: ~의 주위에(주위를 도는 운동 상태)

around: ~의 주위에(주위에 정지한 상태)

about: ~의 주위에(막연한 주변, 여기저기)

    The earth moves round the sun.

    We sat around the bonfire.

    He walked about the park.

to: ~로(도착지점을 표시)

for: ~방향으로(행선지나 목적지를 표시)

from: ~에서(출발지점을 표시)

toward: ~의 방향으로(막연한 목표를 표시)

    He has gone to England.

    He left Seoul for L.A.

    The train is for Busan.

    He started from Seoul

    He bowed toward England.

2) '때'를 나타내는 전치사

at: 시각이나 시점 등 짧은 시간을 나타낸다(몇 시, 몇 분, 밤, 정오, 새벽).

on: 일정한 날짜, 요일, 정해진 시간의 아침, 오전, 오후를 나타낸다.

in: at 보다 긴 시간을 나타낸다(년, 월, 계절, 세기, 아침, 저녁, 오후).

  at six, at night, at noon, at dawn(= daybreak), at midnight.

  on Sunday, on New Year's Day, on May 10th, on the morning of 11th

  in April, in Autumn, in 1945, in the 20th Century

till: '~까지'(어느 때까지의 동작의 계속을 나타낸다)

by: '~까지'(어느 때까지의 동작의 완료를 나타낸다)

before: '전에'(어느 때 이전에 동작의 완료를 나타낸다)

  I will stay here till five.

  I will come here by five.

  I will be at that restaurant till you come.

  I will finish my work by five.

  I usually finish work before six.

in: '~이 지나면'(시간의 경과를 나타낸다. 미래시제가 중심임)

within: '~이내에'(일정한 기간이내를 나타낸다)

after: '~후에'(과거부터)

  She will be back in a few days.

  Cancer will kill him in a few weeks.

  He will come back within a couple of days.

  He came back after few days.

3) 원인/이유의 전치사

for: ~때문에

The boss will blame you for neglecting your job.

from: 직접적인 원인(피로, 부상, 과로 등에 의한)

of: 행위의 원인(~으로: 사망, 병)

He fell ill from drinking too much.

He died from overwork.

4) 원료/재료의 전치사

of: '~으로 만들어 지다'[물리적 변화 – 형태는 변해도 질은 변하지 않는 경우]

from: '~으로 만들어 지다[화학적 변화 – 형태와 질이 모두 변하는 경우]

in: 표현방법. 수단. 재료

The bridge is built of wood.

The house was made of wood.

Wine is made from grapes.

Beer is made from barley.

This picture is painted in oils.

You must write letters in ink.

Speak in English.

Look at the woman in white.

5) 수단/도구의 전치사

by: '~에 의해서'(행위자). '~을 타고'(운송수단)

with: '~을 가지고, ~으로'(도구)

through: '~을 통하여'(중개, 매개수단)

The novel was written by Hemingway

He traveled by train.

He cut bread with knife.

Write it with a pen.

I looked at the moon through a telescope.

We get knowledge through books.

Exercise

A. 문장에서 전치사와 한 묶음이 되는 것에 밑줄을 치세요.

1. The USB in the box is expensive.

2. She went to the post office.

3. They usually play soccer at the school.

4. I haven't seen my son in one year.

B. 빈 칸에 알맞은 전치사를 써 넣으세요.

1. I don't have a pen to write (   ).

2. Candy is (   ) Austria

3. He will meet me (   ) Sunday.

4. I will be back (   ) five o'clock.

5. There are a lot of books (   ) the desk.

6. The police station is (   ) the corner of the street.

7. The chair is made (   ) wood.

Numbers & Calendar

SUNDAY	MONDAY	TUESDAY	WEDNESDAY	THURSDAY	FRIDAY	SATURDAY
		1	2	3	4	◐ 5
		NEW YEAR'S DAY				
6	7	8	9	10	11	● 12
13	14	15	16	17	18	◑ 19
20	21	22	23	24	25	26 ○
27	28	29	30	31		
	MARTIN LUTHER KING, JR. DAY					

first	second	third	fourth	fifth
sixth	seventh	eighth	ninth	tenth
eleven	twelve	thirteen	fourteen	fifteen
sixteen	seventeen	eighteen	nineteen	twenty
thirty	forty	fifty	sixty	seventy
eighty	ninety	hundred	thousand	million

January	February	March	Apri
May	June	July	August
September	October	November	December

Sunday	Monday	Tuesday	Wednesday
Thursday	Friday	Saturday	

January is the first month of the year.

Linda: Do you have new plans for your health?

Andrew: Yes. I made my plan. It is January, the first month of the year. How about you?

Linda: I bought a winter swimming ticket. It costs 200$ for three months.

Andrew: How often do you go to the swimming center?

Linda: I go there on Monday, Wednesday and Friday. Three times a week.

Andrew: It will be good for your health. I bought a monthly exercise ticket. I paid 40$ for a month. I usually go to the center after work.

The tree is _____ years old.

I live on the _____ floor.

A: What month is it?

B: It is _____.

A: What day is it?

B: It is _____.

Vocabulary Test

11 _____   12 _____   13 _____

14 _____   15 _____   20 _____

40 _____   90 _____   100 _____

1,000 _____   1,000,000 _____

1월 _____   2월 _____   3월 _____   4월 _____

5월 _____   6월 _____   7월 _____   8월 _____

9월 _____   10월 _____   11월 _____   12월 _____

월요일 _____   화요일 _____   수요일 _____   목요일 _____

금요일 _____   토요일 _____   일요일 _____

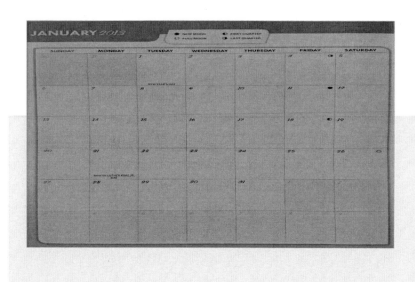

_____

_____

> 의미: 동사의 뜻을 그대로 가지고 있으며, 문장에서 다른 품사처럼 쓰인다.
> 역할: 문장에서 명사, 형용사, 부사처럼 쓰인다.
> 형태: to + 동사원형
> 부정사 부정: 부정사 바로 앞에 부정어를 둔다.

1. 명사적 용법

1) 주어의 역할

To live long is the desire of all men.

To know oneself is difficult.

To work hard is the best way to success.

2) 목적어의 역할(타동사의)

He promised to go there.

He promised me to return at there.

She wants to study English.

3) 보어의 역할

To live is to suffer. (주격보어)

To see her is to love her.

Our wish is to preserve peace.

You have to persuade him to help the poor child. (목적격보어)

She allowed me to play with it.

We all expected him to come here.

4) 명사구(의문사 + to 부정사)

I don't know where to go.

I don't know when to do it.

I don't know whom to go with.

I wondered how to contact them.

I don't know whether to go or turn back.

5) 진주어/진목적어로서

To make ourselves understood is not easy.

      → It is not easy to make ourselves understood.

To work hard is the best way to success.

      → It is the best way to success to work hard.

I make to get up at six every morning a rule.

      → I make it a rule to get up at six every morning.

6) 동격

His ambition, to be a pilot, was never fulfilled.

He has one aim, to make money.

2. 형용사적 용법

1) 한정적 용법

I have no friend to help me.

He is not a person to break his promise.

He is the very man to do this work.

I have no family to look after me.

I bought a book to read on the plane.

There is no time to lose now.

I have a letters to write.

He has many children to look after.

2) 서술적 용법(보어역할)

He seems to be honest. (주격보어)

He appears to be honest. (주격보어)

I chanced to meet her in my walk. (주격보어)

I knew him to be diligent.

I told him to do his best.

* 'be + to 원형동사'의 용법: 이때 'to + 원형동사'는 보어가 된다.

(1) 예정(~할 예정이다 = be due to, be scheduled to)

We are to meet him here.

The meeting is to be held tomorrow.

He is to make a speech next Monday.

(2) 의무/명령(~해야 한다.)

You are to start at once.

You are to obey the law.

(3) 가능(~할 수 있다): 주로 부정문이나 수동태에 사용된다.

Nothing was to be seen.

My house is to be seen from the station.

(4) 운명(~할 운명이다 = be destined to, be doomed to, be fated to)

The poet was to die young.

He was never to see his wife again.

(5) 목적/의도(~하고자 하다 = intended to): 주로 조건절에서 쓰인다.

If you are to succeed, you must work hard.

If you are to catch the train, you had better hurry.

3. 부사적 용법

1) 목적: 동작의 목적을 나타낸다. '~하기 위해서'의 뜻으로 해석

We eat to live, not live to eat.

He raised his right hand to ask a question.

He works hard to succeed in life.

2) 결과: 동작의 결과를 나타낸다.

He lived to see his great-grandchildren.

He grew up to be a great poet.

He worked hard only to fail.

He left his home, never to return.

3) 원인: 감정을 나타내는 동사나 형용사 다음에 오는 부정사는 원인을 나타내며, '~하니', '~해서'의 뜻으로 번역된다.

I am very glad to see you.

I feel sorry to hear of his failure.

He was happy to see his wife again.

I was surprised to find him dead.

She wept to see the sight.

4) 이유, 판단의 근거: '~을 보니', '~을 하다니'로 해석

He is a happy man to have such a good son.

He must be a fool to say such a thing.

He cannot be rich to ask you for some money.

What a foolish he is to believe such a thing!

How foolish I was to trust him!

5) 조건: '만일 ~이면'

To hear him speak English, one would take him for an American.

I should be glad to go with you.

6) 양보: '~할지라도', '비록 ~하여도'

To see it, you would not believe it.

To do his best, he could not succeed in it.

4. 원형부정사('to'가 없이 동사원형만 쓰는 경우)

1) 사역동사 다음에 원형부정사가 쓰인다. 이 때 원형부정사는 목적보어가 된다.

종류: have, make, let, (help)

Father made me turn off the radio.

I will have him wash the car.

He made me do it.

He let her attend the party.

I will help you (to) do the work. (영국식에서는 to를 쓰기도 한다)

2) 지각동사 다음에도 원형부정사가 쓰인다. 이 때 원형 부정사는 목적보어가 된다.

종류: see, hear, feel, watch, listen to, smell

I heard her play the piano in the concert.

I saw him enter the house.

I did not notice him go upstairs.

They observed the birds come back to their nests one by one.

They listened to me speak.

I felt myself tremble with the cold.

5. 부정사의 의미상의 주어

1) 주어가 부정사의 의미상의 주어인 경우

I expect to pass the examination.

He longed to get the prize.

I want to read this novel.

2) 목적어가 부정사의 의미상의 주어인 경우

I expect you to pass the examination.

He told me to work hard.

I advise you to stop smoking.

He allowed me to do so.

He proved it to be true.

3) 의미상의 주어가 '일반인'일 때는 명시하지 않는다.

It is not easy (for us) to learn a foreign language.

4) 사람의 성질이나 특징을 나타내는 형용사 다음에 오는 부정사의 의미상의 주어는 'of + 목적어'를 쓴다.

종류: kind, good, generous, nice, foolish, wise, careful, careless, rude, stupid, silly, polite, bad, cruel.

It is rude of you to speak in that way.

It is very kind of you to say so.

A. 아래 문장에서 부정사를 확인하고, 그 용법(명사, 형용사, 부사)을 표시하세요.

1. To see is very important in life.

2. I don't have time to read the book.

3. He wants to have lunch with him.

4. I don't know wat to do.

5. We have to do our best to win the game.

6. I am glad to see you again.

B. 각 문장에서 밑줄 친 부정사의 의미상의 주어를 확인하세요.

1. Tom wanted <u>to see</u> me yesterday.

2. It is very kind of you <u>to say</u> so.

3. It is very hard for him <u>to get up</u> early in the morning.

4. They told me <u>to meet</u> you here.

5. The man stepped aside for the lady <u>to pass</u>.

C. 문장에 알맞은 것을 고르세요.

1. I saw him (to enter, enter) the classroom.

2. It is impossible (for me, of me) to swim in the river.

3. Jane had him (to finish, finish) the computer game.

4. Let me (look at, to look at) the bag.

5. Do you know what (do, to do) next?

Classroom

textbook	eraser	ruler
calculator	board	bulletin board
bookshelf	screen	projector
stand up	sit down	take notes

open your book	read page seven
close your book	listen to the question
raise your hand	give the answer
work in group	hand in your homework
answer the questions	check your answers
turn off the lights	turn on the projector

Open your books.

Teacher: Open your books to page 20.
Who would like to read it?

Andrew: Can I read it?

Teacher: O.K. Let's listen together.

— — — — — — — — — — — .

Teacher: Thanks. Now, summarize it.

Linda: I already summarized it.

Teacher: Good! Could you share it with Andrew.

Linda: Yes.

Teacher: Linda! Could you pass out these handouts.

Andrew: Can I take two copies for Jane. She is absent today.

Teacher: Yes, you can.

There are ———, ———, and ——— in the classroom.
The professor often use the ——————.

A: Is there a/an —————— in your classroom?
B: Yes there is a/an —————— in my classroom.

A: Make classroom action expressions!?
B: ———————————!

Vocabulary Test

교과서 _____ 지우개 _____ 자 _____

계산기 _____ 칠판 _____ 게시판 _____

책장 _____ 스크린 _____ 프로젝터 _____

일어나세요 _____ 앉으세요 _____ 메모하세요 _____

책을 펴세요 _____ 7쪽을 읽으세요 _____

책을 덮으세요 _____ 질문을 들으세요 _____

손을 드세요 _____ 답을 주세요 _____

그룹으로 공부 하세요 _____

숙제를 제출 하세요 _____

질문에 대한 답을 하세요 _____

답안을 점검하세요 _____

전등을 끄세요 _____

프로젝터를 켜세요 _____

_____

_____

동명사(Gerund)

의미: 동사의 뜻을 그대로 가지고 있으며, 문장에서 다른 품사처럼 쓰인다.

역할: 문장에서 동사적 성질을 갖고, 명사 역할을 한다.

형태: 동사원형 + ing

동명사 부정: 동명사 바로 앞에 부정어를 둔다.

1. 동명사의 역할

1) 주어

Travelling by car is very interesting.

Seeing is believing.

2) 목적어

She began crying bitterly.

I don't like swimming in the river.

She is proud of being a beauty. (전치사의 목적어)

I am fond of swimming. (전치사의 목적어)

3) 보어

My hobby is collecting foreign stamps.

My dream is meeting the poet.

It is throwing your money away.

* 동명사와 현재분사의 구별

　현재 분사: 상태나 동작을 나타내어 '~하고 있는'의 뜻

　동명사: 목적이나 용도를 나타내며 '~하기 위하여'의 뜻

a sleeping baby = a child who is sleeping

a sleeping car = a car used for sleeping

a waiting lady = a lady who is waiting

a waiting room = a room for waiting

2. 동명사의 의미상의 주어

의미상의 주어가 문장 주어와 같을 때는 생략하고, 문장주어와 다를 때는 그 의미상의 주어를 써 주어야 한다. 그러나 문장주어와는 다르지만 그 문장의 목적어와 같을 때는 생략한다.

1) 문장주어와 동일할 때

I am not ashamed of being poor.

He is proud of being a scholar.

2) 문장주어와 다를 때

I insist on his going there.

I insist on my son going there.

3. 동명사의 시제

동명사의 형태는 단순동명사와 완료동명사로 나뉜다. 단순동명사는 그 시제가 술부의 시제와 같거나 하나 더 나아간 미래의 시제이며, 완료 동명사는 술부의 동사보다 하나 앞선 시제이다.

1) 단순동명사

He is proud of being bold.
> = He is proud that he is bold.

He was proud of being bold.
> = He was proud that he was bold.

He is sure of passing the examination.
> = He is sure that he will pass the examination.

2) 완료동명사

I regret having been lazy.
> = I regret that I have been(was) lazy.

He regretted having done so.
> = He regretted that he had done so.

I never heard of such a thing having been done.
> = I never heard that such a thing had been done.

4. 동사에 따른 목적어 형태(동명사와 부정사)

1) 부정사와 동명사 둘 다를 목적어로 취하는 동사
attempt, begin, cease, continue, intend, like, love, omit, start

It continued raining (to rain) all day.

I like taking (to take) a nap after lunch.

I love watching(to watch) TV.

* 목적어가 동명사 또는 부정사 일 때 의미가 달라지는 경우

stop + 동명사(~하는 것을 멈추다): I stopped smoking.

stop + 부정사(~하기 위해 멈추다): I stopped to smoke.

remember + 동명사(~한 것을 기억하다): I remember meeting him.

remember + 부정사(~할 것을 기억하고 있다): I remember to meet him.

forget + 동명사(~한 것을 잊어버리다): I forgot posting the letter.

forget + 부정사(~할 것을 잊어버리다): I forgot to post the letter.

try + 동명사(시험 삼아 ~하다): He tried moving the piano.

try + 부정사(~하려고 시도하다, 노력하다): He tried to move the piano.

go on + 동명사(계속해서 ~하다): He went on talking about his life.

go on + 부정사(쉬었다가 다시 계속하다): He went on to talk about his life.

2) 동명사만을 목적어로 취하는 동사
admit, appreciate, avoid, consider, deny, enjoy, escape, e finish, keep, mind, postpone, quit, remind, suggest

You should quit smoking.

Everyone enjoys singing a song.

She finished reading the novel this morning.

3) 부정사만을 목적어로 취하는 동사

agree, appear, ask, choose, decide, demand, desire, expect, hope, learn, manage, plan, pretend. promise, propose, refuse, seem, tend, want, wish

He promised me not to tell a lie.

He decided to study hard.

I expect to be promoted to manager soon.

5. 동명사의 관용적 용법

It is no use ~ing = It is of no use + to 부정사: '~해도 소용없다'

It is no use crying over spilt milk.

= It is of no use to cry over spilt milk.

It goes without saying that ~: '~은 말할 필요조차 없다'

It goes without saying that honesty is the key to success.

cannot help ~ing = cannot but + 원형: '~하지 않을 수 없다. ~할 수밖에 없다'

I could not help laughing at the funny sight.

= I could not but laugh at the funny sight.

feel like ~ing: '~하고 싶은 생각이 들다'

I feel like making a trip somewhere.

be busy ~ing: '~하는데 분주하다. ~하느라고 바쁘다'

He was busy preparing for the exam.

go ~ing: ~하러 가다(주로 여가 활동을 언급할 때 쓰인다)

I went fishing yesterday.

look forward to ~ing: '~을 기대하다'

I am looking forward to seeing you again.

A. 아래 문장에서 동명사를 확인하고, 그 역할(주어, 보어, 목적어)을 표시하세요.

1. Talking with him is very interesting.

2. The students often avoid answering their teacher's questions.

3. My mother stopped me from making a mistake.

4. Her hobby is gardening.

5. Thanks for inviting me.

B. 아래 문장에서 알맞은 것을 선택하세요.

1. He decided (to buy, buying) the car.

2. All of them don't want (to play, playing) soccer.

3. I don't mind (to study, studying) with him.

4. My brother is busy (to do, doing) his project.

5. We can't help (to laugh, laughing) at his jokes.

6. He promised (to let, letting) me know what the teacher said.

7. Could you show me a (to sleep, sleeping) bag?

Colors

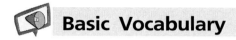

Basic Vocabulary

silver   gold

red   orange

yellow   green

blue   purple

pink   gray

brown   white

black

What color does it stand for?

Charles: I like your yellow sweater.
You look good in yellow.

Andrew: Yellow is my favorite color. Did a singer sing our national anthem.

Charles: Yes he did. Look! There are many national flags behind the stage.

Andrew: All of them are beautiful. Every flag has its own special color.

Charles: The color of the flags stands for the country's identity.

Andrew: What colors does your country stand for?

Charles: I think they are white and blue.

Andrew: White stands for purity and blue stands for peace.

Pattern Practice

My favorite color is _____.

_____ is the symbol of _____.

A: What color is it?

B: it is _____.

A: What color makes you comfortable _____?

B: It is _____.

은색 _____   금색 _____

빨강색 _____   오렌지색 _____

노란색 _____   초록색 _____

파랑색 _____   보라색 _____

핑크색 _____   회색 _____

갈색 _____   흰색 _____

검정색 _____

Describing A picture

_____

_____

분사(Participle)

의미: 동사의 뜻을 그대로 가지고 있으며, 문장에서 다른 품사처럼 쓰인다.

역할: 문장에서 동사적 성질을 갖고, 동사 또는 형용사처럼 쓰인다.

형태: 동사원형 + ing or 동사원형 + ed

종류: 현재분사, 과거분사

* 동사 역할: 진행형, 완료형, 수동태에서 쓰일 때

He is studying English.

The book was written by me.

They have worked for five years.

1. 분사의 의미

1) 현재분사: 진행(~하고 있는), 능동 또는 사역(~시키는, ~하게 하는)을 나타냄.

A rolling stone gathers no moss.

People living in the country generally live long.

Look at that falling leaves.

A growing number of young people seek a job.

2) 과거분사: 완료나 상태(~한, ~해버린), 수동(~된, ~당한, ~받은)을 나타냄.

Look at the mountain covered with snow.

A wounded soldier lay bleeding.

The broken computer is mine.

* 의미 비교

It was an exiting game.

An exited spectator starts yelling.

He was exited by the news of the victory

The baseball game was exiting.

The story is interesting.

He was interested in the subject.

It is a surprising event.

I was surprised to hear the news.

His speech was boring

I was bored to hear his speech.

2. 분사의 용법

1) 한정적 용법

(1) 전위 수식: 분사가 단독으로 명사 앞에서 그 명사를 수식한다.

Don't wake up the sleeping child.

Spoken language and written language are two aspects of language.

(2) 후위 수식

분사가 단독으로 쓰이더라도 대명사를 수식할 때.

Those swimming in the pond are my classmates.

Of those invited, all but Tom came to the party.

분사가 보어, 목적어, 부사(구) 등의 부속어구와 같이 쓰이면 형용사구가 되어 후위 수식한다.

The child sleeping there is Mary.

Once there lived a man named Robin Hood.

2) 서술적 용법

(1) 주격보어로 쓰일 때

He sat reading a novel.

He stood looking at the picture.)

He sat surrounded by his children.

He came in quite exhausted.

(2) 목적격보어로 쓰인다.

I saw him going into the room.

I felt myself watched all the time.

I heard him well spoken of.

I couldn't make myself understood in English.

3. 분사구문

복문(두 개 이상의 절로 만들어진 문장)에서 분사로 시작하는 절에서 사용되며, 사용된 분사는 접속사 + 주어 + 동사가 포함되어 있는 것

1) 때: when, while, as, after

Walking along the street, I met an old friend of mine.

→ While I was walking along the street, I met an old friend of mine.

Left alone, I began to read.

→ When I was left alone, I began to read.

* 다음의 경우에는 being과 having been은 생략되는 것이 보통이다.

(1) 분사구문이 수동태일 경우(과거분사 앞에 놓일 때)

As he was wounded in the legs, he could not walk.

→ (Being) Wounded in the legs, he could not work.

As I had been pleased with the article, I bought it.

→ (Having been) Pleased with the article, I bought it.

(2) 형용사, 명사, 부사, 현재분사 앞에 놓일 때

(Having been) Lazy all his life, he had nothing to offer to his son.

As he is an expert, he knows how to do it.

→ (Being) An expert, he knows how to do it.

(Being) Only a poor student, I hadn't money enough to buy it.

As I was reading a book, he came in.

→ (Being) Reading a book, he came in.

2) 원인, 이유: as, because, since

Having nothing to do, I went to bed.

> → As I had nothing to do, I went to bed.

Not knowing what to do, he just stood and looked.

> → As he did not know what to do, he just stood and looked.

* 분사구문의 부정: 분사 앞에 not 또는 never를 붙인다.

3) 조건: if

Meeting her, I shall be very glad.

> → If I meet her, I shall be very glad.

Read carelessly, Some books will do more harm than good.

> → If they are read carelessly, some books will do more harm than good.

4) 양보: though, although, even if

Young, she has much experience.

> → Though she is young, she has much experience.

Born of the same parents, they bear no resemblance.

> → Though they were born of the same parents, they bear no resemblance.

5) 부대상황

(1) 동시동작: while, as(~하면서)

Smiling brightly, she shook hands with me.

        → She smiled brightly and shook hands with me.

Raising his hands, he stood up and answered.

        → As he raised his hands, he stood up and answered.

Singing and dancing together, we had a good time.

        → As we sang and danced together, we had a good time.

(2) 연속동작: and + 동사(그리고 ~하다)

We started in the morning, arriving in Seoul at seven.

        → We started in the morning, and arrived in Seoul at seven.

He picked up a stone, throwing it at a dog.

        → He picked up a stone, and threw it at a dog.

4. 분사의 시제

분사는 단순형 분사와 완료형 분사로 나눌 수 있다. 단순형 분사는 주절의 시제와 같은 시제를, 완료형 분사는 주절의 시제보다 하나 앞선 시제를 나타낸다. 즉, 주절의 동사가 현재이면 완료형 분사의 시제는 과거 또는 현재완료이며, 주절의 동사가 과거이면 완료형 분사의 시제는 과거완료가 된다.

Living in the country, I am very healthy.

        → As I live in the country, I am very healthy.

Having finished the work, I have much free time now.

        → As I have finished the work, I have much free time now.

Written in plain English, this book is very easy to read.

    → As this book is written in plain English, it is very easy to read.

Scolded, she cried.

    → As she was scolded, she cried.

5. 독립분사구문

분사구문의 의미상의 주어가 주절의 주어와 다를 경우에는 의미상의 주어를 따로 써주어야 한다. 이와 같이 분사구문의 의미상의 주어가 주절의 주어와 다른 분사구문을 독립분사구문이라고 한다.

After the sun had set, we gave up looking for them.

    → The sun having set, we gave up looking for them.

As it was fine, we went for a walk.

    → It being fine, we went for a walk.

We shall start tomorrow, if (the) weather permits.

    → We shall start tomorrow, weather permitting.

Though I admit what you say, my friends still don't believe it.

    → I admitting what you say, my friends still don't believe it.

He was reading a book, and his wife was knitting beside him.

    → He was reading a book, his wife knitting beside him.

Exercise

A. 밑줄 친 분사가 수식하고 있는 것을 확인하세요.

1. The old man <u>sitting</u> on the bench looks tired.

2. The <u>broken</u> computer will be fixed.

3. I couldn't believe the <u>shocking</u> news.

4. All of the <u>invited</u> students enjoyed the show.

5. The meeting <u>scheduled</u> for this evening is canceled.

B. 문장에 알맞은 형태를 고르세요.

1. She left the door (unlocking, unlocked).

2. The (retiring, retired) man visited the company.

3. They found the (losing, lost) child in the park.

4. The game was very (exciting, excited).

5. The building (painting, painted) green is a shopping center.

C. 밑줄 친 분사를 풀어쓰세요.

1. Seeing me, he ran away.

2. Finishing the homework, She takes a nap.

3. Being sick, Tom didn't attend the meeting.

4. Following this road, you will find the police station.

5. Being sick, I finished the project.

Animals

fox	wolf	tiger
leopard	lion	hyena
elephant	deer	squirrel
rabbit	bat	giraffe
donkey	horse	pony
buffalo	camel	cow
pig	kangaroo	zebra
bear	pander	monkey
chimpanzee	gorilla	hamster
hippopotamus	rhinoceros	

Look at the monkey!

Linda: Look at the monkeys!

Andrew: All of them look sleepy.

Linda: Shall we throw bananas into the cage?

Andrew: No, don't do that. It will hurt them. Let's go to see buffaloes.

Linda: Good. Where are they?

Andrew: They will be a wild place over there.

Linda: Wow! They look big and wild. I have never seen them before.

Andrew: I saw them at Yellow Stone national park. There were many buffaloes in the field without guarding.

Linda: You did! The park is the first national park in USA. Is it a nice place to visit?

Andrew: Yes. The park is huge. Many travellers usually stay there several days to see the park.

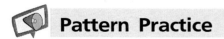 **Pattern Practice**

I like _____ because _____.
I don't like _____ because _____.

A: What is the biggest animal in the world?
B: I think it is the _____.

A: What kinds of animals are there in the zoo?
B: There are _____ _____ _____ in the zoo.

Vocabulary Test

여우 _____   늑대 _____   호랑이 _____

표범 _____   사자 _____   하이에나 _____

코끼리 _____   사슴 _____   다람쥐 _____

토끼 _____   박쥐 _____   기린 _____

당나귀 _____   말 _____   조랑말 _____

버펄로 _____   낙타 _____   소 _____

돼지 _____   캥거루 _____   얼룩말 _____

곰 _____   판다 _____   원숭이 _____

침팬지 _____   고릴라 _____   햄스터 _____

하마 _____   코뿔소 _____

Describing A Picture

_____

_____

수동태(Passive)

> 의미: 의사 전달에 있어 문장주어의 관점에 따른 문장표현 방법으로, 일반적으로 많은 문장들은 능동문으로 사용되고 있으나, 때때로 주어가 동작이나, 행위를 받는 문장을 사용할 때가 있다. 이를 수동태 문장이라 한다.
>
> 역할: 주어가 동작을 받는 문장으로서 각종 보고서나 전달문의 문장으로 사용되고, 때때로 강조를 하고자 할 때 사용한다.
>
> 일반구조: 주어 + be동사 + 과거분사 + by 목적어

1. 태의 전환

능동태와 수동태: 능동태는 동작을 하는 쪽에, 수동태는 동작을 받는 쪽에 중점

1) 능동태를 수동태로 바꿀 때

(1) 능동태의 목적어가 수동태의 주어가 된다.

(2) 능동태의 동사는 be + 과거분사의 형태로 바뀐다.

(3) 능동태의 주어는 by + 목적격의 형태로 부사구를 이룬다.

He wrote this letter.

→ This letter was written by him.

All the people in the world admire Kennedy.

→ Kennedy is admired by all the people in the world.

* 주의: 자동사는 수동태가 될 수 없다.

lie, sit, rise, die, arrive, work, wait, belong, consist, (dis)appear, exist, occur, happen, originate

The cost of transportation has been risen with the price of gasoline.(×)

* 주의: 타동사이지만 수동태로 전환할 수 없는 동사

resemble, have, meet, lack, escape, belong to, let.

He resembles his father.

　　　　→ His father is resembled by him.(×)

He escaped death.

　　　　→ Death was escaped by him.(×)

2. 수동태의 시제: 수동태의 be동사는 능동태 동사의 시제와 일치한다.

The hotel was built (by people) in 1994.

	현재	과거	미래
단순형	is built	was built	will be built
완료형	has been built	had been built	will have been built
진행형	is being built	was being built	(will be being built)

* 주의: 조동사가 있을 경우에 조동사는 그대로 둔다. 그러나 will, shall은 인칭에 맞게 바꾸어 주어야 한다.

You must read the book.

　　　　→ The book must be read by you.

Jack can build the house.

　　　　→ The house can be built by Jack.

3. 주의할 수동태

1) 4형식의 수동태: 능동태 4형식에 있는 직접목적어와 간접목적어를 주어로 선택할 수 있다.

Henry gave me these books.
> → I was given these books by Henry.
> These books were given me by Henry.
> These books were given to me by Henry.

He asked me the question.
> → I was asked the question by him.
> The question was asked me by him.
> The question was asked of me by him.

* 직접목적어를 주어로 하여 전치사를 수반할 때. 직접목적어를 주어로 하면 간접목적어는 보류목적어(Retained Object)가 된다. 이 때 보류목적어 앞에는 to, for, of 등의 전치사가 놓인다.
(send, tell, lend, give : to/make, buy : for/ask, require, inquire : of)

* 주의: make, buy, write, sing, send, pass, get, bring 등의 수여동사는 직접목적어만 수동태의 주어가 될 수 있다.
I wrote him a letter. → A letter was written him by me.(O)
> He was written a letter by me.(×)
She sang me a song. → A song was sung me by her.(O)
> I was sung a song by her.(×)

* 주의: spare, save, envy, kiss, answer 등의 수여동사는 간접목적어만 수동태의

주어가 될 수 있다.

They envied him his luck.

　　　→ He was envied his luck by them.(O)

　　　　His luck was envied him by them.(×)

He kissed her good night.

　　　→ She was kissed good night by him.

2) 능동태 5형식을 수동태로 고치면 2형식이 된다.

이 때 막연한 일반인을 나타내는 we, you, one, they, people, somebody, someone 등은 수동태에서 생략되는 경우가 많다.

I painted the gate green. → The gate was painted green by me.

They elected Kennedy President.→ Kennedy was elected President. (by
　　　them)

They elected him chairman. → He was elected chairman. (by them)

3) 보어가 원형부정사인 수동태: 술부동사가 지각동사 또는 사역동사일 경우, 원형부
정사는 수동태에서 'to 부정사'로 바뀐다.

He made me do it.

　　　→ I was made to do it by him.

We saw him enter the room.

　　　→ He was seen to enter the room. (by us)

We heard him sing.

　　　→ He was heard to sing by us.

4. 의문문의 수동태

1) 의문사가 없는 의문문

Did you plant this tree?

        평서문 → You planted this tree.

        수동태 → This tree was planted by you.

        의문문 → Was this tree planted by you?

2) 의문사가 있는 의문문

What did he do?

        평서문 → He did what. (비문장)

        수동태 → What was done by him. (비문장)

        의문문 → What was done by him?

5. 수동태가 많이 쓰이는 경우

1) 능동태의 주어가 분명치 않을 때

He was killed in the war.

The continent was discovered about 300 years ago.

2) 능동태의 주어가 막연한 일반인을 나타낼 때

Spanish is spoken in Mexico, too.

The rule was seldom observed.

3) 능동태의 주어보다 수동태의 주어에 더 관심이 클 때

The child was run over by a car.

Mr. Reagan was elected President again.

The bed was not slept in.

4) 수동태의 의미가 거의 없이 자동사로 느껴지는 경우

He was drowned while swimming in this river.

Her eyes were drowned in tears.

He was suddenly taken ill.)

My University is located on the hill.

He was born in 1970.

He is ashamed of what he did.

6. 수동태에서 'by' 이외의 전치사를 쓰는 경우

1) 'at'을 쓰는 동사: surprise, shock

I am surprised at the news.

2) 'in'을 쓰는 동사: interest

I am interested in the movie.

3) 'with'을 쓰는 동사: cover, satisfy, please

I am satisfied with the result.

A.아래 문장이 능동태문장인지, 수동태 문장인지 확인하세요.

1. Tom bought Jane a ring.
2. The shopping mall will be opened soon.
3. He has waited his children for two hours.
4. Many students has respected the teacher.
5. The book was published.

B. 아래 문장을 수동태로 바꾸세요.

1. They broke the window yesterday.
2. Shakespeare wrote Hamlet.
3. The policeman arrested the thief.
4. I will finish the project.
5. He gave me a gift.

C. 빈 칸에 알맞은 전치사를 쓰세요.

1. I am interested (   ) English.
2. My father satisfied (   ) his work.
3. The ground is covered (   ) snow.
4. He was surprised (   ) the news.

Clothing

shirt	blouse
sweater	jacket
vest	bra
pants	shorts
skirt	underpants
running shorts	uniform
suit	dress
nightgown	bathrobe
coat	raincoat
trench coat	pajamas

How about this green T-shirt?

Robert: I can't find my blue T-shirt?

Olivia: Did you look in the closet?

Robert: I already looked there. It will be very fit for me today.

Olivia: How about this green T-shirt? It will be good for you.

Robert: Ok, I will take it. I don't have enough time.
We had better hurry up.

Olivia: Many people will participate the campaign.
All of them will wear casual clothes.

Robert: We have to bring raincoats. It will be raining at the afternoon.

Olivia: I will also bring a jacket.

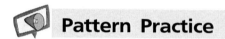

Could you show me new _____?

I will take the _____.

A: I am looking for _____?

B: You can find _____ over there.

A: Where did you buy _____?

B: I bought _____ at Lotte store.

Vocabulary Test

셔츠 _____   블라우스 _____

스웨터 _____   재킷 _____

조끼 _____   브래지어 _____

바지 _____   반바지 _____

스커트 _____   팬티 _____

운동반바지 _____   단체복 _____

정장 _____   원피스 _____

나이트가운 _____   목욕가운 _____

코트 _____   비옷 _____

바바리코트 _____   잠옷 _____

_____

_____

관계사(Relative)

의미: 두 문장을 하나로 연결하지만, 순수 접속사와 달리 선행사가 있다.
역할: 접속사 + 명사 혹은 부사 역할
종류: 관계대명사, 관계부사

1. 관계대명사

주격	소유격	목적격	선행사
who	whose	whom	사람
which	whose/of which	which	사물/동물
that	-	that	사람/사물/동물
what	-	what	(선행사 포함)

1) Who

(1) 주격

He is the man. + He saved the child.

→ He is the man who saved the child.

I employed a man. + He I thought was honest.

→ I employed a man who I thought was honest.

(2) 소유격

This is the gentleman. + His pulse has been stolen.

→ This is the gentleman whose purse has been stolen.

A child is called an orphan. + His parents are dead.

   → A child whose parents are dead is called an orphan.

(3) 목적격

He is the man. + She saved him.

   → He is the man whom she saved.

I employed a man. + I thought him to be honest.

   → I employed a man whom I thought to be honest.

2) Which

(1) 주격

I have a book. + It is very interesting.

   → I have a book which is very interesting.

(2) 목적격

This is the book. + I bought it yesterday.

   → This is the book which I bought yesterday.

(3) 소유격: whose, of which

The house is my uncle's. + Its roof is red.

   → The house whose roof is red is my uncle's.

   → The house of which the roof is red is my uncle's.

3) That

(1) 선행사에 최상급, 서수, the only, the very, the last, the first 등과 같은 강한 한정 어구가 붙을 때나, 선행사가 부정형용사(any, no, all, some, little, few, much)에 의해 수식을 받을 때 관계대명사 who 또는 which 보다 that을 주로 쓴다.

This is the best movie that I have ever seen.

He is the only poet that I know well.

There is no man that doesn't love his own country.

(2) 선행사가 '사람 + 동물', '사람 + 사물'일 때.

Look at the boy and his dog that are running over there.

The driver and the car that fell into the river have not been found.

4) What

선행사를 포함하고 있기 때문에 what = that which, the thing which, all that 등으로 바꿀 수 있다.

(1) 주어절: What I want is your advice. (what = That which)

(2) 보어절: I am not what I used to be. (what = the man that)

(3) 목적어절: I will do what I can. (what = all that)

5) 관계대명사의 두 용법(' , '의 유무에 따라 구분)

(1) 제한적 용법

He had two sons who became doctors.

She is the first love that I loved.

(2) 계속적 용법: 관계대명사가 계속적 용법으로 쓰일 때, 문장의 내용에 따라 접속사 + 대명사(and, but, for, though + 대명사)로 바꾸어 쓸 수 있다.

He had two sons, who became doctors. (who = and they)

We trust him, who is very honest. (who = for he)

This book, which is old, is of great value to me. (which = though it)

* 관계대명사 what와 that은 계속적 용법이 없다.

I cannot understand, what he says.(×)

He has a horse, that runs very fast.(×)

6) 관계대명사의 생략(목적격 관계대명사)

(1) 동사의 목적어가 될 때

This is the man (whom) I like best.

The movie (which) I saw yesterday was interesting.

He is the only poet (that) I know well.

(2) 전치사의 목적어가 될 때

This is the man (whom) you spoke of the other day.

This is the hotel (which) we stopped at last time.

2. 관계부사

선행사를 가지면서, 접속사와 부사의 구실을 한다. 이 때 선행사 시간(때), 장소, 이유, 방법을 나타내는 명사이다. 관계부사는 전치사 + which로 바꾸어 쓸 수 있다.

종류: when, where, why, how

1) when: 선행사가 time, day, occasion, season 등의 '때'를 나타낼 때 쓰인다.
이 때 when은 at, in, on, during + which로 바꾸어 쓸 수 있다.

I don't know the time. + It happened then.
→ I don't know the time when it happened. (when = at which)

2) where: 선행사가 place, house, town, village 등의 '장소'를 나타낼 때 쓰인
다. 이 때 where는 in, at, to + which로 바꾸어 쓸 수 있다.

This is the village. + I was born there.
→ This is the village where I was born. (where = in which)

3) why: 선행사가 reason일 때 쓰인다. why는 for + which로 바꾸어 쓸 수 있다.

Tell me the reason. + You did not come for that reason.
→ Tell me the reason why you did not come. (why = for which)

4) how: 방법을 나타내며, 선행사 없이 쓰인다.

This is the way. + It happened in that way.
→ This is (the way) how it happened.
→ This is the way in which it happened.

3. 복합관계사

1) 복합관계대명사

복합관계대명사는 관계대명사 + ever의 형태로서, 자체에 선행사를 포함하고 있으며 (선행사 + 관계대명사), 명사절 또는 부사절로 쓰인다.

종류: whoever, whomever, whosever, whichever, whatever

(1) 명사절을 유도할 때

Whoever comes is welcome. (= Anyone who: ~하는 사람은 누구나)

Give it to whomever you like. (= anyone whom)

Return it whosever address is on it. (= anyone whose)

You may take whichever you like. (= anything that: ~하는 것은 어느 것이나)

I will give you whatever you need. (= anything that: ~하는 것은 무엇이나)

(2) 양보의 부사절을 유도할 때: '누가/누구를/어떤 것을/무엇을 ~한다 할지라도'

Whoever may break this law, he will be punished. (= No matter who)

Whomever you may love, he will desert you. (= No matter whom)

Whichever you may choose, you will be interested in it. (= No matter which)

Whatever happens, I will go. (= No matter what)

2) 복합관계부사

선행사를 자체에 포함하고 있으며 부사절을 유도한다.

종류: wherever, whenever, however

(1) wherever 장소의 부사절: ~하는 곳은 어디든지

　양보의 부사절: ~로(에) …할지라도

　You may go wherever you like. (= at any place where)

　Wherever she is, I will find her. (= No matter where)

(2) whenever 시간의 부사절: ~할 때는 언제나

　양보의 부사절: 언제 ~할지라도

　You may come whenever you like. (= at any time that)

　Whenever you may call on me, you will find me at my desk. (= No matter when)

(3) however 양보의 부사절: 아무리 ~할지라도

　However hard you may try, you cannot do it in a week. (= No matter how)

　However rich a man may be, he should not be idle. (= No matter how)

Exercise

A. 아래 문장에서 관계사와 선행사에 밑줄을 치세요.

1. I know him who lives in Denver.

2. This is the phone which I bought yesterday.

3. He met a man whose son is a singer.

4. This is the only pen that I have.

5. I don't know the time when the shop is open.

B. 두 개의 문장을 하나로 합치세요.

1. This is the book. I want to buy it.

2. This is the town. I was born there.

3. I bought a phone. Its screen is wide.

4. He likes the computer. His father bought him it.

5. I know a man. He works for the company.

C. 빈칸에 알맞은 관계사를 써 넣으세요.

1. Do you know the man (   ) is watching the game?

2. I have a girl friend (   ) father is a professor.

3. I gave my son all the money (   ) I had.

4. Sunday is the day (   ) we go to church.

5. Do you know the reason (   ) he is so happy?

Musical Instruments

Basic Vocabulary

flute	clarinet	oboe
recorder	saxophone	
trumpet	trombone	tuba
violin	viola	cello
guitar	ukulele	mandolin
harp		
drum	cymbals	xylophone
piano	organ	
accordion	harmonica	

Dialogue

My sister is a fan of the band.

Charles: Did you hear about the famous band concert?

Andrew: I didn't. I think the band is great.
My sister is a fan of the band.

Charles: I am going to buy tickets for me and my wife. Tickets are usually cheaper if we get them in advance.

Andrew: I will ask if my sister want to or not. She used to play violin and drum. But, she doesn't play any musical instrument these days. She may be too busy.

Charles: If you want to, you can get tickets at the door.

Andrew: I hope the concert will be successful.

I can play the _____ .
The _____ sound is fantastic!

A: Do you play a musical instrument?
B: Yes. I play the _____ .

A: What is the name of the _____?
B: It is _____ .

플루트 _____   클라리넷 _____   오보에 _____
리코더 _____   색소폰 _____

트럼펫   트럼본 _____   튜바 _____

바이올린   비올라 _____   첼로 _____
기타 _____   우쿨렐레 _____   만도린 _____
하프 _____

드럼 _____   심벌즈 _____   실로폰 _____

피아노 _____   오르간 _____

아코디언 _____   하모니카 _____

Describing A Picture

_____

_____

일치(Agreement)

의미: 영어에서는 주어에 따라서 동사가 단수형인가 복수형인가를 선택하여야 한다.

1. 주어와 동사의 일치

1) 주어의 단수와 복수

My friend lives in Boston.

My brother and sister live in Boston.

2) 명사구나 절이 주어가 되는 경우: 단수로 받는다.

Growing flowers is her hobby. (동명사구)

To live long is the desire of man. (부정사구)

Whether he will agree with me is doubtful. (명사절)

3) and로 연결되는 경우

and로 연결되는 두 개 이상의 명사가 별개의 사람이나 사물이면 복수로, 동일한 사람이나 사물이면 단수로 취급한다.

John and Jim are roommates this semester.

A teacher and scientist is supposed to come.

4) 형용사 every와 each ⇒ 단수를 수식하고, 단수 취급한다.

Every boy and girl is taught to read and write.

Every man, woman, and child needs love.

Each book and magazine is listed in the card catalog.

2. 수량 표시

1) each[one/every one] of + 복수명사 ⇒ 단수 취급

Every one of my friends is here.

One of the most famous films is Gone with the Wind.

Each of the boys has his own desk.

2) a number of + 복수명사 ⇒ 복수 취급
the number of + 복수명사 ⇒ 단수 취급

A number of students were late for class. (a number of = many)

The number of students in the class is fifteen. (~의 숫자)

3) many a + 단수명사 ⇒ 단수 취급

Many a soldier was killed at the field.

3. 수의 일치

1) 'there'로 유도되는 구문의 동사는 주어와 일치시킨다.

There are twenty students in my class.

There's a fly in the room.

2) 회사[단체] 이름, 지명, 학문 명, 유희 등은 단수로 받는다.

Sears is a department store.

Physics is easy for her.

Billiards is usually played by two persons.

3) 시간, 거리, 가격의 표현이 하나의 의미로 쓰일 경우 단수 취급한다.

Eight hours of sleep is enough.

Ten years is a long time to wait.

Five thousand miles is too far to travel.

Ten dollars is too much to pay.

4) 수식 표현은 단수 취급한다.

Two and two[Two plus two] is/equals four.

Five times five is twenty five.

Ten minus five leaves/equals five.

Fifteen divided by three is five

5) 나라 이름이나 그 나라 언어를 나타낼 때: 단수
그 나라 사람들을 나타낼 때: 복수

English is spoken in many countries.

Chinese is his native language.

The English drink tea.

The Chinese have an interesting history.

The Americans are a passionate people.

The Koreans are a peace-loving people.

6) the + 형용사: 복수보통명사

The rich get richer. (= rich people)

The poor have many problems. (= poor people)

the young(젊은 사람들)/the dead(죽은 사람들)

7) 상관 접속사의 일치

(1) either A or B/neither A nor B/A or B ⇒ B에 일치(B가 주어)
John or I am to blame.

(2) not only A but also B ⇒ B/A as well as B ⇒ A에 일치
James, as well as his friends, was injured in the accident.

(3) both A and B ⇒ 복수 취급
Both brother and sister are dead.

8) 집합명사(단일성 강조) ⇒ 단수 취급/군집명사(개별성 강조) ⇒ 복수 취급

My family is large.

All my family are early risers.

The audience was a large one.

The audience were all deeply moved.

9) 항상 복수 취급하는 명사

(1) police, peasantry, clergy, nobility: 정관사와 같이 쓰인다.

The police are on the murderer's track.

The clergy are all kindness to the poor.

(2) people, cattle, poultry: 부정관사도 못 붙이고 복수형으로 쓰이지도 않는다.

Those people are from Canada.

Cattle feed on grass.

10) 형식은 복수이지만, 하나의 단위로 취급해서 단수로 받는다.

Ten years is a long time to wait.

A hundred miles is a long distance.

Five hundred dollars a month is a small sum to him.

11) It is ~ that 강조 구문에서는 강조되는 부분과 일치

It is you that are to blame.

It is I who am fit to do this work.

Exercise

A. 문장에 알맞은 형태를 고르세요.

1. The pen on the desk (is, are) mine.

2. Tom and Bill (live, lives) together in the house.

3. Many a solder (was, were) killed at the war.

4. There (is, are) many people at the room.

5. Either you or I (am, are) supposed to attend the meeting.

6. My family (is, are) all very well.

7. Every boy and every girl in the room (watch, watches) TV.

8. The doctor and artist (is, are) my friend.

9. Each of them (is, are) happy.

10. Mathematics (is, are) my favorite subject.

11. Not only she but also I (like, likes) the teacher.

12. Ten dollars (is, are) is too much to pay.

불규칙동사 형태변화표
수(數) 읽는 법

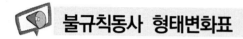

불규칙동사 형태변화표

현재	과거	과거분사
awake	awoke	awoken
be	was/were	been
beat	beat	beaten
become	became	become
begin	began	begun
bend	bent	bent
bite	bit	bitten
break	broke	broken
bring	brought	brought
build	built	built
burn	burned/burnt	burned/burnt
buy	bought	bought
catch	caught	caught
choose	chose	chosen
come	came	come
cut	cut	cut
deal	dealt	dealt
dive	dived/dove	dived/drove
do	did	done
draw	drew	drawn
dream	dreamed/dreamt	dreamed/dreamt
drink	drank	drunk
drive	drove	driven
eat	ate	eaten
fall	fell	fallen
feel	felt	felt
fight	fought	fought

현재	과거	과거분사
fly	flew	flown
find	found	found
forget	forgot	forgotten
freeze	froze	frozen
get	got	got/gotten
give	gave	given
go	went	gone
grow	grew	grown
hang	hung	hung
have	had	had
hear	heard	heard
hide	hid	hidden
hit	hit	hit
hold	held	held
hurt	hurt	hurt
keep	kept	kept
know	knew	known
lead	led	led
leave	left	left
lend	lent	lent
let	let	let
lose	lost	lost
make	made	made
meet	met	met
pay	paid	paid
put	put	put
read	read	read
ring	rang	rung
rise	rose	risen
run	ran	run

현재	과거	과거분사
say	said	said
see	saw	seen
seek	sought	sought
sell	sold	sold
send	sent	sent
shake	shook	shaken
shine	shone	shone
shoot	shot	shot
show	showed	shown
shut	shut	shut
sing	sang	sung
sit	sat	sat
sleep	slept	slept
speak	spoke	spoken
spend	spent	spent
stand	stood	stood
steal	stole	stolen
strike	struck	struck
swim	swam	swum
take	took	taken
teach	taught	taught
tell	told	told
think	thought	thought
throw	threw	thrown
wake	woke/waked	woken/waked
wear	wore	worn
win	won	won
write	wrote	written

수(數) 읽는 법

기 수		서 수	
1	one	1st	first
2	two	2nd	second
3	three	3rd	third
4	four	4th	fourth
5	five	5th	fifth
6	six	6th	sixth
7	seven	7th	seventh
8	eight	8th	eighth
9	nine	9th	ninth
10	ten	10th	tenth
11	eleven	11th	eleventh
12	twelve	12th	twelfth
13	thirteen	13th	thirteenth
14	fourteen	14th	fourteenth
15	fifteen	15th	fifteenth
16	sixteen	16th	sixteenth
17	seventeen	17th	seventeenth
18	eighteen	18th	eighteenth
19	nineteen	19th	nineteenth
20	twenty	20th	twentieth
21	twenty-one	21th	twentieth-first
30	thirty	30th	thirtieth
40	forty	40th	fortieth
50	fifty	50th	fiftieth
60	sixty	60th	sixtieth
70	seventy	70th	seventieth

기 수		서 수	
80	eighty	80th	eightieth
90	ninety	90th	ninetieth

100	one hundred
10,000	ten thousand
100,000	one hundred thousand
1,000,000	one million

Answers

Lesson 1   Exercise

A. 밑줄 친 단어의 품사를 구분하세요.

1. I forgot to book a <u>ticket</u> for the movie.   (명사)
2. I am going to meet him <u>at</u> the coffee shop.   (전치사)
3. Mary <u>and</u> Tom look very happy.   (접속사)
4. He showed her an <u>expensive</u> computer.   (형용사)
5. English is not <u>so</u> easy for me.   (부사)
6. The man invited <u>my</u> sister yesterday.   (대명사)

B. 아래 문장에서 밑줄 친 동사를 자동사와 타동사로 구분하세요.

1. He <u>smiles</u> at me.   (자동사)
2. We <u>made</u> a reservation.   (타동사)
3. They <u>went</u> to the park in the morning.   (자동사)
4. I <u>found</u> the book difficult.   (타동사)
5. They don't <u>want</u> to take a bus.   (타동사)

C. 아래 문장의 몇 형식 문장인지 구분하세요.

1. The beautiful bird is singing on the tree.   (1형식)
2. I thought it a dog.   (5형식)
3. The man killed himself on Monday.   (3형식)
4. Seoul is the capital of Korea.   (2형식)
5. Could you lend me your pen?   (3형식)

Lesson 2   Exercise

A. 아래 문장의 종류를 구분하세요.

   평서문, 의문문, 명령문, 감탄문

1. What a kind man he is!   (감탄문)
2. Did you meet him yesterday?   (의문문)
3. Let him go.   (명령문)
4. Is she a teacher?   (의문문)
5. The program is very useful.   (평서문)

B. 아래문장들을 부정문으로 만드세요.

1. My uncle <u>was</u> very diligent.
    was not

2. My sister <u>watched</u> the TV show yesterday.
    did not watch

3. They <u>paint</u> the roof white.
    do not paint

4. William <u>sent</u> Linda the jewelry box.
    did not send

5. I <u>can</u> do it.
    can not

C. 아래문장들을 의문문으로 만드세요.

1. He is interested in politics.
   → **Is he interested in politics?**

2. Susan is from America.
   → **Is Susan from America?**

3. She likes to talk on the phone.
   → **Does she like to talk on the phone?**

4. Birds sing in the forest.
   → **Do birds sing in the forest?**

5. She will do her best tomorrow.
   → **Will she do her best tomorrow?**

Lesson 3   Exercise

A. 아래 문장에서 명사에 밑줄을 치고, 그 종류(보통, 집합, 물질, 추상, 고유)를 쓰세요.

1. The <u>boy</u> wants to be a good <u>doctor</u>.   (보통, 보통)
2. He ordered a <u>cup</u> of <u>coffee</u>.   (보통, 물질)
3. The <u>audience</u> have to pay extra <u>money</u> for the <u>concert</u>.   (보통, 물질, 보통)
4. There are many <u>people</u> in <u>Seoul</u>.   (보통, 고유)
5. <u>Honesty</u> is very important.   (추상)

B. 아래 문장에서 밑줄 친 명사가 셀 수 있는 명사인지(가산), 아닌지(불가산)를 표시하세요.

1. There are many <u>churches</u> in the city.   (가산)
2. He is a smart <u>student</u>.   (불가산)
3. Jane loves <u>Tom</u>.   (불가산)
4. She went to the <u>Busan</u>.   (불가산)

5. We paid much <u>money</u>.   (불가산)
6. <u>Glass</u> is easy to break.   (불가산)
7. We had much <u>snow</u> last winter.   (불가산)
8. The traveller wanted some <u>water</u>.   (불가산)
9. The <u>team</u> won the game.   (가산)
10. <u>Knowledge</u> is very important.   (불가산)

C. 아래문장에서 밑줄 친 부분을 바르게 고치세요. 필요하면 a/an을 첨가하세요.

1. There are many **potatoes** in the shop.
2. Could you lend me **a car**?
3. I don't understand **English**.
4. He come from **Japan**.
5. **Milk** is good for health.
6. The roof is covered with **snow**.
7. There are three **knives** on the table.
8. They took care of three **babies**.

Lesson 4 Exercise

A. 괄호 안에 알맞은 인칭대명사를 써 넣으세요.

1. This question is very difficult for (목적격 대명사; me, …).
2. This pen is (소유대명사; mine, …).
3. She sent (목적격; me, …) a letter.
4. (I, you, we, they) work for Samsung.
5. The man asked me (소유격; my, …) address.

B. 괄호 안에 알맞은 대명사를 써 넣으세요.

1. The girl showed me a red sweater, but I don't like (it).
2. This dog is stronger than (목적격; me, …).
3. They were proud of (목적격; me, …) for winning the game.
4, He said the bag was (소유대명사; mine, …).
5. My mother bought me blue neck ties, and I really like (it).
6. If you need a pen, I will give (one) to you.

C. 아래 문장에서 밑줄 친 'it'의 쓰임을 구분 하세요.

1. <u>It</u> is snowing outside.   (비 인칭 주어)
2. How far is <u>it</u> from here to the mall.   (비 인칭 주어)
3. Tom bought a car and he drove <u>it</u> to the school. (a car)

4. How far is <u>it</u> from here to the mall.   (비 인칭 주어)

5. I tried to open the box, but <u>it</u> was impossible.   (the box)

6. <u>It</u> is already five.   (비 인칭 주어)

Lesson 5   Exercise

A. 밑줄 친 동사의 종류를 구분하세요. (be동사, 조동사, 일반동사)

1. He <u>lives</u> in Seoul.   (일반동사)

2. I <u>believe</u> you made a mistake.   (일반동사)

3. The man <u>became</u> a famous artist.   (일반동사)

4. The foreigner <u>can</u> speak Korean.   (조동사)

5. She has <u>finished</u> her project.   (일반동사)

6. Edward <u>was</u> a computer programer.   (be동사)

B. 밑줄 친 동사의 과거형을 쓰세요.

1. I <u>have</u> a lot of books.   (had)

2. She <u>writes</u> Harry Potter.   (wrote)

3. They <u>think</u> he is a doctor.   (thought)

4. Many people <u>want</u> to see the game.   (wanted)

5. The player <u>hit</u> the ball.   (hit)

6. I <u>read</u> a history novel.   (read)

C. 밑줄 친 동사의 시제를 구분하세요.

1. <u>Have</u> you ever been to America?   (현재완료)

2. John <u>is staying</u> in Seoul.   (현재진행)

3. She could not sleep well, because she <u>had had</u> much tea.   (과거완료)

4. My brother <u>will be</u> there about 2:30.   (미래)

5. The teacher <u>has been waiting</u> for his son.   (현재완료진행)

Lesson 6   Exercise

A. 아래 문장에서 알맞은 것을 고르세요.

1. Eliot (could, <u>**must**</u>) be on vacation this week.

2. He (might, <u>**have to**</u>) meet me at the theater.

3. The boy (<u>**can**</u>, could) attend the English class in the evening.

4. You (could, <u>**should**</u>) do obey your parents.

5. They insist that he (<u>should</u>, will) be sent there.

6. (<u>May</u>, Must) I borrow your pen?

7. (<u>Can</u>, Will) I ask you a question?

8. (May, <u>Shall</u>) we dance?

9. (<u>Would</u>, Should) you help me?

10. (<u>Could</u>, May) you be quite, please.

Lesson 7   Exercise

A. 밑줄 친 단어 앞에 관사가 필요하면 써 넣으세요.

1. Dog is <u>a faithful</u> animal.

2. I need to <u>a teacher</u> to help me.

3. I think she is <u>a music</u> dancer.

4. <u>Water</u> is very important.

5. One of my friends lives in <u>Seoul</u>.

6. We should know <u>life</u> is not so long.

B. 밑줄 친 부정관사의 의미를 보기에서 찾아 쓰세요.

보기) one, per, some, a certain

1. They talked about <u>a</u> movie.   (a certain)

2. There is <u>an</u> apple on the table.   (one)

3. My son usually drink two glasses of milk <u>a</u> day. (per)

4. You had better take a rest for <u>a</u> day or two.   (one)

5. My mother will stay here for <u>a</u> time.   (some)

C. 빈 칸에 알맞은 관사를 써 넣으세요.

1. (**The/a**) caw is a useful animal

2. I don't have (**a**) driver's license.

3. Yesterday, I bought a USB, but I lost (**the**) USB.

4. Please, open (**the**) door.

5. (**–**) sun rises in the east.

6. He caught me by (**the**) hand.

Lesson 8   Exercise

A. 밑줄 친 형용사가 꾸며주는 명사를 고르세요.

1. I was late at the meeting because of <u>heavy</u> **traffic**.
2. **Something** <u>spicy</u> was put into her soup.
3. There is a ugly <u>broken</u> **car** on the street.
4. I met **somebody** <u>famous</u> at the mall.
5. My <u>favorite</u> **sport** is baseball.

B. 밑줄 친 형용사가 설명해 주고 있는 단어(명사 또는 대명사) 또는 구를 고르세요.

1. **The city** is <u>fantastic</u>.
2. My mother always made **me** <u>happy</u>.
3. I know **he** is very <u>smart</u>.
4. I think they believed **him** <u>honest</u>.

C. 문장에 알맞은 것을 고르세요.

1. I have (a few, **a little**) breakfast in the morning.
2. He spent (**many**, much) days doing his project.
3. There is (many, **much**) snow in this winter.
4. How (**many**, much) pictures did you take in USA.
5. I don't have (a few, **a little**) knowledge about it.
6. The man want to get (**a few**, a little) notebooks.

Lesson 9   Exercise

A. 밑줄 친 부사가 꾸며주는 것을 찾으세요.

1. The doctor talks <u>very</u> **fast**.
2. <u>Unfortunately</u>, **he was absent**.
3. He is **old** <u>enough</u> to take a trip by himself.
4. I **slept** <u>deeply</u> yesterday.
5. My son **learns** language <u>quickly</u>.

B. 주어진 부사(구)를 문장에 알맞게 써 넣으세요.

1. She **usually** gets up early in the morning.
2. He is rich **enough** to buy the car.
3. Tom can speak English **well**.

4. I used to go shipping with my husband **all the time**.

5. I am **really** happy to meet you.

C. 밑줄 친 단어의 뜻을 쓰세요.

1. The bus arrived ten minutes <u>late</u>.   (늦게)

2. I haven't seen him <u>lately</u>.   (최근에)

3. The man is working <u>hard</u>.   (열심히)

4. He <u>hardly</u> ever go to church.   (거의 ~ 않다)

5. The cat can jump <u>high</u>.   (높이)

6. It is a <u>highly</u> interesting movie.   (상당히)

Lesson 10   Exercise

A. 문장에서 접속사가 연결하고 있는 것에 밑줄 치세요.

1. I want to buy <u>apples</u> and <u>tomatoes</u> at the shop.

2. We should <u>take this bus</u> or <u>wait for next one</u>.

3. <u>Tom lost his wallet</u>, but <u>his wife found it at the park</u>.

4. <u>To be</u> or <u>not to be</u>, that is a question.

B. 빈칸에 알맞은 단어를 써 넣으세요.

1. (**Both**) she (**and**) I were satisfied with the result.

2. (**Either**) John or Jane will be a first player.

C. 접속사가 이끄는 절에 밑줄을 치세요.

1. He told me that <u>he couldn't take the position</u>.

2. My wife asked if <u>I wanted to have lunch at home</u>.

3. Mike thought that <u>I had made a mistake</u>.

4. I wonder weather <u>Linda told a lie</u>.

5. That <u>she is honest</u> is clear.

Lesson 11   Exercise

A. 문장에서 전치사와 한 묶음이 되는 것에 밑줄을 치세요.

1. The USB <u>in the box</u> is expensive.

2. She went <u>to the post office</u>.

3. They usually play soccer <u>at the school</u>.

4. I haven't seen my son **in one year**.

B. 빈 칸에 알맞은 전치사를 써 넣으세요.
1. I don't have a pen to write (**with**).
2. Candy is (**from**) Austria
3. He will meet me (**on**) Sunday.
4. I will be back (**in**) five o'clock.
5. There are a lot of books (**on**) the desk.
6. The police station is (**at**) the corner of the street.
7. The chair is made (**of**) wood.

Lesson 12   Exercise

A. 아래 문장에서 부정사를 확인하고, 그 용법(명사, 형용사, 부사)을 표시하세요.
1. **To see** is very important in life.   (명사)
2. I don't have time **to read** the book.   (형용사)
3. He wants **to have** lunch with him.   (명사)
4. I don't know wat **to do**.   (명사)
5. We have to do our best **to win** the game.   (부사)
6. I am glad **to see** you again.   (부사)

B. 각 문장에서 밑줄 친 부정사의 의미상의 주어를 확인하세요.
1. **Tom** wanted to see me yesterday.
2. It is very kind of **you** to say so.
3. It is very hard for **him** to get up early in the morning.
4. They told me **to meet** you here.
5. The man stepped aside for **the lady** to pass.

C. 문장에 알맞은 것을 고르세요.
1. I saw him (to enter, **enter**) the classroom.
2. It is impossible (**for me**, of me) to swim in the river.
3. Jane had him (to finish, **finish**) the computer game.
4. Let me (**look at**, to look at) the bag.
5. Do you know what (do, **to do**) next?

Lesson 13   Exercise

A. 아래 문장에서 동명사를 확인하고, 그 역할(주어, 보어, 목적어)을 표시하세요.

1. <u>Talking</u> with him is very interesting.   (주어)
2. The students often avoid <u>answering</u> their teacher's questions. (목적어)
3. My mother stopped me from <u>making</u> a mistake.   (목적어)
4. Her hobby is <u>gardening</u>.   (보어)
5. Thanks for <u>inviting</u> me.   (목적어)

B. 아래 문장에서 알맞은 것을 선택하세요.

1. He decided (<u>to buy</u>, buying) the car.
2. All of them don't want (<u>to play</u>, playing) soccer.
3. I don't mind (to study, <u>studying</u>) with him.
4. My brother is busy (to do, <u>doing</u>) his project.
5. We can't help (to laugh, <u>laughing</u>) at his jokes.
6. He promised (<u>to let</u>, letting) me know what the teacher said.
7. Could you show me a (to sleep, <u>sleeping</u>) bag?

Lesson 14   Exercise

A. 밑줄 친 분사가 수식하고 있는 것을 확인하세요.

1. The <u>old man</u> <u>sitting</u> on the bench looks tired.
2. The <u>broken</u> <u>computer</u> will be fixed.
3. I couldn't believe the <u>shocking</u> <u>news</u>.
4. All of the <u>invited</u> <u>students</u> enjoyed the show.
5. The <u>meeting</u> <u>scheduled</u> for this evening is canceled.

B. 문장에 알맞은 형태를 고르세요.

1. She left the door (unlocking, <u>unlocked</u>).
2. The (retiring, <u>retired</u>) man visited the company.
3. They found the (losing, <u>lost</u>) child in the park.
4. The game was very (<u>exciting</u>, excited).
5. The building (painting, <u>painted</u>) green is a shopping center.

C. 밑줄 친 분사를 풀어쓰세요.

1. <u>Seeing</u> me, he ran away.
   When he saw ~,

2. <u>Finishing</u> the homework, she takes a nap.
   After she finished ~,
3. <u>Being</u> sick, Tom didn't attend the meeting.
   Because he was sick,
4. <u>Following</u> this road, you will find the police station.
   If you follow ~,
5. <u>Being</u> sick, I finished the project.
   Though he was sick,

Lesson 15   Exercise

A.아래 문장이 능동태문장인지, 수동태 문장인지 확인하세요.

1. Tom bought Jane a ring.   **(능동태)**
2. The shopping mall will be opened soon.   **(수동태)**
3. He has waited his children for two hours.   **(능동태)**
4. Many students has respected the teacher.   **(능동태)**
5. The book was published.   **(수동태)**

B. 아래 문장을 수동태로 바꾸세요.

1. They broke the window yesterday.
   → **The window was broken by them yesterday.**
2. Shakespeare wrote Hamlet.
   → **Hamlet was written by Shakespeare.**
3. The policeman arrested the thief.
   → **The thief was arrested by the policeman.**
4. I will finish the project.
   → **The project will be finished by me.**
5. He gave me a gift.
   → **I was given a gift by him.**

C. 빈 칸에 알맞은 전치사를 쓰세요.

1. I am interested (**in**) English.
2. My father satisfied (**with**) his work.
3. The ground is covered (**with**) snow.
4. He was surprised (**at**) the news.

Lesson 16　Exercise

A. 아래 문장에서 관계사와 선행사에 밑줄을 치세요.
1. I know <u>him</u> who lives in Denver.
2. This is <u>the phone</u> which I bought yesterday.
3. He met <u>a man</u> whose son is a singer.
4. This is the only <u>pen</u> that I have.
5. I don't know <u>the time</u> when the shop is open.

B. 두 개의 문장을 하나로 합치세요.
1. This is the book. I want to buy it.
　→ This is the book which I want to buy.
2. This is the town. I was born there.
　→ This is the town where I was born.
3. I bought a phone. Its screen is wide.
　→ I bought a phone whose screen is wide.
4. He likes the computer. His father bought him it.
　→ He likes the computer which his father bought him.
5. I know a man. He works for the company.
　→ I know a man who works for the company.

C. 빈칸에 알맞은 관계사를 써 넣으세요.
1. Do you know the man (who) is watching the game?
2. I have a girl friend (her) father is a professor.
3. I gave my son all the money (that/which) I had.
4. Sunday is the day (when) we go to church.
5. Do you know the reason (why) he is so happy?

Lesson 17　Exercise

A. 문장에 알맞은 형태를 고르세요.
1. The pen on the desk (<u>is</u>, are) mine.
2. Tom and Bill (live, <u>lives</u>) together in the house.
3. Many a solder (<u>was</u>, were) killed at the war.
4. There (is, <u>are</u>) many people at the room.
5. Either you or I (<u>am</u>, are) supposed to attend the meeting.
6. My family (is, <u>are</u>) all very well.

7. Every boy and girl in the room (watch, **watches**) TV.
8. The doctor and artist (**is**, are) my friend.
9. Each of them (**is**, are) happy.
10. Mathematics (**is**, are) my favorite subject.
11. Not only she but also I (**like**, likes) the teacher.
12. Ten dollars (**is**, are) is too much to pay.